I0808033

EXPLORING THE LIFE, MYTH, AND ART OF THE ANCIENT NEAR EAST

CIVILIZATIONS OF THE WORLD

EXPLORING THE LIFE, MYTH, AND ART OF THE ANCIENT NEAR EAST

M. KERRIGAN, A. LOTHIAN, P. VITEBSKY

ROSEN PUBLISHING

This edition published in 2017 by:
The Rosen Publishing Group, Inc.
29 East 21st Street
New York, NY 10010

Library of Congress Cataloging-in-Publication Data

Names: Kerrigan, Michael, 1959- author. | Lothian, Alan, co-author. | Vitebsky, Piers, co-author.
Title: Exploring the life, myth, and art of the ancient Near East / Michael Kerrigan, Alan Lothian, Piers Vitebsky.
Description: New York : Rosen Publishing, 2017. | Series: Civilizations of the world | Audience: Grades 7 to 12. | Includes bibliographical references and index.
Identifiers: LCCN 2016015415 | ISBN 9781499463972 (library bound) Subjects: LCSH: Middle East—Civilization—To 622—Juvenile literature. | Iraq—Civilization—To 634—Juvenile literature. | Middle East—Social life and customs—Juvenile literature. | Mythology, Middle Eastern—Juvenile literature. | Art, Middle Eastern—History—Juvenile literature.
Classification: LCC DS62.2 .K385 2017 | DDC 935—dc23
LC record available at https://lccn.loc.gov/2016015415

Manufactured in China

Contents

THE ANCIENT NEAR EAST

To the few travellers who hurried quickly across the desert, the wind-swept, sand-choked mounds they passed were scarcely worth a second glance. Occasionally, the more daring of the region's inhabitants would come to search among the debris, looking for baked mud bricks with which to build or repair their own simple homes, but usually the mounds were left strictly alone.

No one knew that these spoil-heaps had once been great cities, each housing thousands of people and bearing such names as Babylon, Nineveh, Ur and Ashur. The farmers of rural southern Iraq had enough to concern them, scratching a living in this backwater of the Ottoman Empire and contending with the regular floods that ravaged their settlements and the ancient mounds alike.

In the year 1616, one curious traveller, an Italian aristocrat called Pietro della Valle, dug out a few bricks from a hump the local Arabs called Tell al Muqayyar ("the mound of pitch"), and which in more prosperous times had been known as Ur. The bricks were marked with writing "in certain unknown characters", and once back in Italy, della Valle sent them around as scholarly curiosities to some of his more thoughtful friends.

At first, the inscribed mud bricks attracted only modest interest. But a new era of enquiry was dawning in Europe and during the eighteenth century a few more travellers risked the journey along the old river valleys of the Tigris and the Euphrates, and a few more savants, fascinated by what they had read in the Bible of such strange places, tried to make sense of the baffling marks.

It all took time: the puzzle yielded only slowly, its solution the work of generations of scholars. Yet the discovery, when it came, was as dramatic as could be. Beneath those neglected mounds lay nothing less than evidence of the origins of civilization. Its story was plainly written out in della Valle's "unknown characters", not hidden, just forgotten. And with the combined effort of linguists and excavators, it would be remembered once again.

Left: **Three rampant goats, their heads covered in gold foil, rise from a bowl carried by deities in this 18th-century BC votive gift. This very early bronze piece was found in Larsa, in southern Iraq.**

Opposite: **The ancient city of Ashur was strategically situated on the banks of the Tigris. The river was vital for life in the region, providing transport as well as irrigating crops.**

The partially restored ziggurat at Ur is a reminder of Mesopotamia's sometime magnificence. The most impressive monument built during the reign of Ur-Namma (2112–2095BC), it consisted of a series of platforms and staircases, on top of which was a temple.

"Mesopotamia" – a Greek word meaning "between the rivers" – refers to the once-fertile area centred around the Tigris and Euphrates valleys. Until well into the nineteenth century, the only information about this part of the ancient Near East was to be found in the Bible and, to a lesser extent, in a few classical texts. These mostly made reference to the ancient empires of Babylon, Assyria and nearby Canaan. The handful of kings and rulers whose names had survived the years were generallyrepresented – at least in the Bible – as odious, tyrannical leaders. As a result, their long-remembered murderous habits provided Hebrew prophets with many a moral tale.

The city of Babylon itself was flourishing as late as 331BC, when Alexander the Great arrived to help himself to the riches of the Persian Empire he had just ruthlessly overcome. After Alexander's arrival, however, Babylon's fortunes turned and the city fell into decline, and by the beginning of the Christian era there was little left of its former glory but a mound of dust and debris, although the desolate city remained inhabited until as late as the fourteenth century AD.

Such decay was baffling to early travellers, brought up on biblical tales of ancient magnificence. Today we know enough about early building techniques to understand what happened. The main construction material in the cities was unfired mud brick, which was cheap and easy to work with, but required constant maintenance. Every winter, roofs would need a new mud layer and floors would require re-laying, and the run-off material, along with the general detritus of everyday life, went into the streets, gradually causing the city's ground level to rise.

If catastrophe struck, by means of war or earthquake, a devastated city quickly became a shapeless heap, on which subsequent generations could rebuild. The result was the characteristic "tell" of the Middle East, a low mound concealing the remains of many millennia of occupation.

By the seventeenth century, a few European visitors had begun to dig around in some of the better-known ruins. Mostly, they hoped to find an inscription or two that might link an ancient site with biblical accounts; and so it was that their discoveries, the first examples of cuneiform writing, arrived back in Europe – to the general bafflement of the continent's scholars.

The bafflement increased as more expeditions brought back yet more samples of writing. Clearly, these wedge-shaped marks preserved on hardened clay were the key to the societies that had once inhabited the ruined mounds, but it would not be until the nineteenth century that people once more learned how to read them. Only then did archaeologists realize that these first civilizations had formed the basis for subsequent cultures throughout the Middle East and Europe.

The cracking of the cuneiform code was a long and complex task involving scholars all over Europe. By the 1850s, the core of the task had been accomplished and scholars were able to extract at least some meaning from many of the thousands of inscriptions so far unearthed.

They called the language "Babylonian" as the tablets dated from the late third millennium BC, when the Babylonian Empire was at its height, and the existence of any older culture remained, for a time, unsuspected. The first clue that there had been something earlier came from an incongruity between the spoken language and the written script. "Babylonian" (known as "Akkadian") was a Semitic tongue, kin to present-day Hebrew and Arabic. But the script seemed to have been created for a language with an entirely different structure – perhaps by the region's first civilized inhabitants.

By the late nineteenth century, this theory was beyond doubt. In the ruins of Lagash and Nippur, archaeologists opened the treasure troves of a long-forgotten civilization. Among the first things they discovered was its name: Sumer. And as if to make up for millennia of oblivion, the old mounds were generous with their secrets – the Nippur expedition alone unearthed some 30,000 inscribed tablets which were probably written in the city's scribal school.

Many tablets were simply records of the daily activities of an ancient city, but others were more exciting, revealing stories of great kings and heroes, songs of love and war, tales of quarrelling and capricious gods. Such accounts provided valuable insights into these forgotten cities, revealing the tales and histories of the first civilizations that the world had ever known.

This detail from a relief discovered at Nimrud's North West Palace shows tribute bearers and an intricate cuneiform inscription from the reign of Ashurnasirpal II (883–859BC).

The First Cities

Archaeology, of necessity, progresses backwards, moving layer by layer from the present down to the distant past. However, thanks to more than a century of heavy spadework and diligent scholarship, we can reconstruct a less inverted picture of humankind's urban dawn.

Some time during the fourth millennium BC, the people now known as the Sumerians, living in the land between the Tigris and Euphrates rivers, developed writing. They were not the area's first inhabitants: there are traces of human habitation going back as far as Paleolithic times, around 100,000 years ago. Much later, around 7000BC, the region was almost certainly the scene of the so-called Neolithic Revolution, when humans took the huge step from nomadic hunting and gathering to settled agriculture, and over the next few thousand years substantial villages began to spring up.

Following the invention of agriculture, the pace of change was astonishingly fast. After a long reliance on a few simple stone implements, human technology quickly expanded to include such vital adjuncts as pottery, ploughs, chariots and copper-working. And the invention of the sail turned the area's vast tangle of rivers into something of a rapid-transport network.

But for the first real cities to come into existence, another incentive was required. Rainfall in these regions of southern Iraq was too low to support large-scale agriculture and, in order to sustain the already-substantial population, organized irrigation became necessary. Such organization needed government; and government made urban living possible. By about 3300BC the Sumerian city-state was thriving, with almost the entire population living in urban centres, whose walls deterred attacks from nomad bands or rival cities.

In this way, the Sumerians set the pattern of urban existence for thousands of years to come, with the lives of the pastoralists and farmers

This lifelike bronze statue of a basket-carrier from the end of the 3rd millennium BC indicates advances in metalworking, which flourished in Sumer at this time.

revolving around the administrative and religious centres they served with their labour. Sumer's total population may have reached as much as half a million at its height, yet each individual city-state was on a small, almost intimate scale and, in addition to earthly rulers, each city had its own tutelary deity, involved in the community's day-to-day life as well as in ritual ceremony.

Almost from their very beginning, the new cities were home to an even newer profession: the scribe. It was probably administrative necessity that led to the invention of writing. With trade and government both on a scale never seen before, something more than mere human memory was now needed to keep track of things.

In its earliest form, around 3500BC, Sumerian writing was pictographic, a series of tiny images impressed on blocks of slightly damp clay by the scribes. The early writing had groups of images in "boxes" arranged in columns and it was not until around 2000BC that the writing began to flow in horizontal lines. Over time the pictograms evolved into the abstract, angular impressions that characterize cuneiform script. The word cuneiform actually means "wedge shaped", and refers to the patterns pressed into the clay by a carefully sharpened, cut reed.

It did not take the scribes long to appreciate that the potential of the new invention went far beyond mere administrative convenience. Already by 2500BC cuneiform script was used for literature as well as everyday bookkeeping; hymns, poetry, literary contests and even great epics all found a place in the libraries of city-rulers' courts. They can still be read today, for clay tablets, having been kiln-baked, are remarkably durable. However, much is fragmentary, and much is still mysterious. Even after more than a century of modern cuneiform scholarship, translation is often difficult and sometimes impossible.

The Ancient Near East

The main cities of ancient Mesopotamia generally developed along the fertile river valleys of the Euphrates and Tigris. As the cities became established, an intricate system of irrigation canals was also constructed.

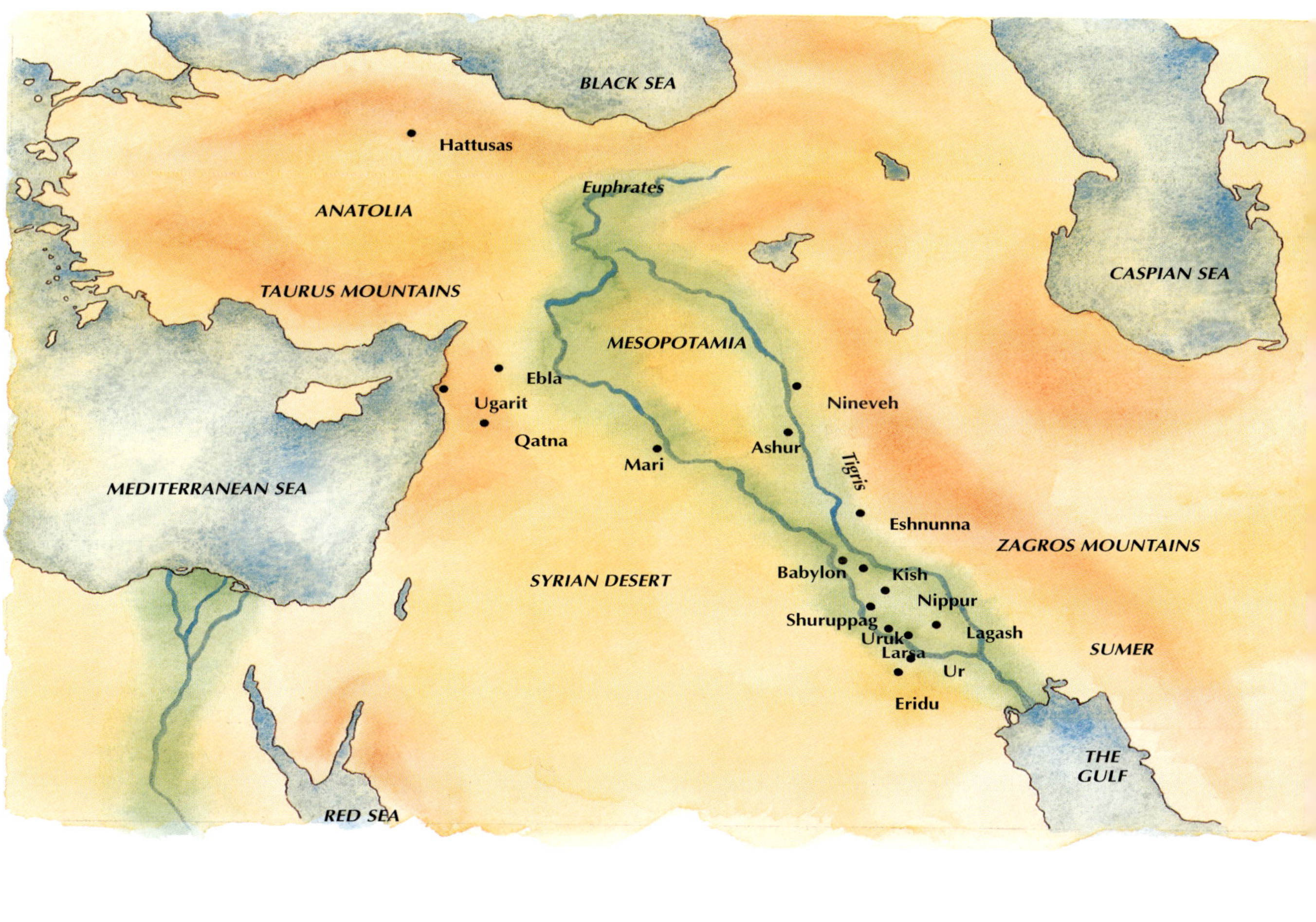

This cast copper head of an Akkadian ruler, thought to be Sargon or Naram-Sin, was found near the Ishtar Temple at Nineveh.

The Dominance of the Akkadians

Those first written tablets and their contents would long outlive the culture that produced them, as would the cuneiform script itself. For the Sumerians – the word "Sumer" refers to what is now southern Iraq – were not the only people living in the area. They were joined by the Semitic-speaking Akkadians, who lived alongside them for a very long time and adopted the complex Sumerian script for their own writings. It was this borrowing of script which caused problems for scholars later on. Although a cuneiform logogram might mean the same thing in both Sumerian and Akkadian, it represents a different word in each language, and even experts can find it difficult to decide in which language a phrase was written.

However, there are more written records in Akkadian than Sumerian, as towards the end of the third millennium bc, Akkadian increasingly began to take over as the dominant language of power. Around 2300bc, an Akkadian empire centred around the northern city of Agade sprang up. It overwhelmed the Sumerian city-states and ended the precarious, jostling independence that most of them had hitherto enjoyed. The new empire created by Sargon the Great, a ruler famous for his prowess on the battlefield – lasted barely two centuries. But, despite the subsequent revival of Sumerian culture and political power, the Akkadian tongue achieved a dominance that it was to retain for well over a thousand years.

TIMELINE

Many aspects of daily life now taken for granted, such as writing, mathematics and the use of unstamped coins, were invented by these ancient Near Eastern civilizations. The origins of these concepts are impossible to date precisely as they almost certainly developed over time, and so are given here in the era in which there is the first firm evidence of their existence.

4000–3000BC

Baked clay ewe's head dating from c.3000BC

c.3500 Development of first cities
c.3400 Sumerians invent writing and develop sexagesimal system (sixty-minute hour)

Cultural developments
Wheel, cylinder seal, writing, mathematics, monumental architecture

Thus the dynasties of Babylon wrote their story in Akkadian, and their fables too, which often re-told and elaborated upon Sumerian originals. The language – at least in its scribal form – was remarkably stable from the death of Hammurabi, in 1750bc, right up to the fall of Babylon to Persia in 539bc. Under Persian control Aramaic had become the administrative language of government, but even so Akkadian continued in written use until the first century ad.

As the strength of Babylon waned, that of Assyria, centred around the city of Ashur, waxed. Gradually, often as a result of the infiltration and disruption caused by waves of nomadic invaders into Mesopotamia, the Assyrian Empire expanded. By 800bc it had become the region's greatest power, eventually ruling over Babylon itself. Even the Assyrians recognized the cultural superiority of the Babylonian dialect over their common language and, for much of its existence, Akkadian served as the language of trade and diplomacy for the entire region and beyond. It was understood throughout most of the so-called fertile crescent – the arc of cultivated land that cradled the Earth's earliest civilizations and which curved around the littoral of the eastern Mediterranean from the shallow valleys of the Tigris and Euphrates rivers to its western limb in Egypt.

Elsewhere, knowledge of Akkadian was an invaluable asset in the first epoch of regular long-distance commerce. Such journeying necessitated communication, and probably accounts for the common themes present in Akkadian literature and in that of other traditions – the Old Testament, for example, or Greek mythology such as the Odyssey. For, as time passed, the cities of Mesopotamia were joined by partners and rivals in Canaan, Syria and Anatolia.

3000–2000BC

c.3000 Possibly the first mention of flood story but date is disputed
c.2600–1850 Flourishing of Sumerian city-states

Cultural developments
Metal weapons, refinement of cuneiform script, city-states, ziggurats

2000–1000BC

c.1894–1550 First Dynasty of Babylon
c.1742–1460 Hittite Old Kingdom
c.1500 Rise of city of Ashur and the Assyrian Empire
c.1500–1200 Golden age of Ugarit
c.1460–1200 Hittite Empire

Cultural developments
Cavalry, coins, brass, Aramaic language

This Hittite stele found in Marash, Turkey, shows a scene from family life, with a woman spinning and a scribe at work writing in cuneiform

1000–700BC

An 8th-century basalt Assyrian stele of warriors from Tell Ahmar

c.883–612 Assyrian domination of Mesopotamia
c.705–612 Nineveh becomes capital of Mesopotamia

700–500BC

c.600 Twelve signs of the Zodiac identified by Babylonians
689 Babylon destroyed by King Sennacherib of Assyria
c.668–627 The fullest extant text of the Epic of Gilgamesh is written on twelve Akkadian tablets in the library of Nineveh
639–625 Neo-Babylonian Empire
539 Conquest of Babylon by Cyrus of Persia
c.539–331 Persian Empire dominates Mesopotamia

Detail of a relief from the palace at Nineveh built by Ashurbanipal (668–627BC), showing Assyrian huntsmen

A 9th-century BC statue of the Canaanite god of storms, Baal-Hadad, and Ishtar, known to the Canaanites as Astarte, goddess of love and war. She became the most important female deity of the ancient Near East.

The Discovery of the Canaanites

Mesopotamia's trading relationships covered most of the known world, communicating via Syria with Egypt and the whole Mediterranean, north through Anatolia to the Black Sea and, by 2000BC, by ship to the great Harappan civilization 2,500 kilometres to the east in the Indus valley. One trading partner was certainly the Canaanite port of Ugarit on the coast of Syria. The people of Ugarit spoke a northwestern Semitic language, related to Hebrew and Akkadian, and used their own alphabetic script to write it. The city's records, in the form of clay tablets uncovered during several digs in the 1930s, have provided the best insight into Canaanite religion. Until these discoveries, the only sources of knowledge of the beliefs of the Canaanites had been a few, fragmentary Greek texts and Old Testament accounts of "Baal-worship".

The word "Baal" simply means "lord", and was used by different Canaanite cities to refer to their own, particular tutelary deity: Baal-Sidon, for example, was the guardian of the city of that name. Ugaritic texts include lengthy mythological narratives and complex rituals, which frequently combine the actions of gods and Canaanite kings from a mythical past. There was also a place for well-known Mesopotamian deities: Astarte, for example, appears to have been the Canaanite version of the Sumerian goddess Inana.

Mesopotamian ideas were spread by commerce as much as conquest. From about 1900BC, there were thriving communities of Assyrian merchants in Anatolia, not ruling over the local population but living in equality among them,quietly paying taxes from the considerable profits of their trade. They were drawn to Asia Minor by its rich supplies of copper, silver and gold. Careful records that they left behind show that, in exchange for these metals, they sold high-quality Mesopotamian woollen textiles (which included carpets, rugs and woven cloth), and they even imported tin (for bronze-making) from as far afield as Afghanistan. The Assyrians also brought with them their perception of the world – ideas, religious and otherwise – and of course their use of the written word.

The Hittites and the Old Testament

There are around forty references to the Hittites in the Old Testament. Exactly which ones relate to representations of the great flowering of the Hittite Empire in the fourteenth century BC, and which to the so-called Neo-Hittites who followed them, is not always certain.

At the very beginning of the Old Testament, in Genesis, "Ephron the Hittite" gives Abraham a piece of land, including the cave that will be his burial place. Abraham's grandson Esau took a Hittite wife, while Exodus and Joshua frequently mention "the Hittites" as among the luckless inhabitants of Canaan destined to be "ruthlessly destroyed" during the Israelite conquest. However, the Hittites are not always portrayed as enemies of the Jews. Later, "Uriah the Hittite", who is a soldier of King David, has Uriah's death arranged so that he can enjoy the favours of his wife.

These biblical citations – together with a few scant references in ancient Egyptian and Assyrian records – amounted to all that was known of the mighty Hittite kingdom. It was considered legendary by many scholars, until 1906 when excavations at Boghazkoy in Turkey proved otherwise. In fact, the Hittites exercised a loose hegemony over much of northern Canaan during the thirteenth century BC, when Joshua supposedly led the Israelite invasion, and it is likely that Hebrews and Hittites would have met frequently during the period. However, scholars still hotly debate the date and nature of Joshua's conquest as well as its historicity.

Many of the references in the Old Testament are probably to the Neo-Hittite successor states to the Hittite Empire which occupied northern Syria from 1200bc, following the empire's collapse in Anatolia. The Neo-Hittites had a separate identity, and also a different official language – Luwian – replacing the older Hittite tongue.

Hattusas, capital of the Hittite Empire, was destroyed and abandoned shortly after 1200BC.

Invaders from the North

The Assyrian traders' Anatolian hosts were Hurrian or Hattic tribal peoples. By the second millennium BC a new group of invaders had established themselves in the region – the people known to history as the Hittites, who originated from modern-day southern Russia. They took their name, and that of their capital city Hattusas, from their Hattic predecessors who originated in the Anatolian heartland.

The Hittites were a people to whom literacy came relatively late – the oldest known texts are from the fourteenth century BC. Like the Canaanites, they used the cuneiform writing developed by Sumerian scribes so long before, adapting it yet again to a language utterly different from its originators'.

From the many thousands of clay tablets excavated at Hattusas (now the village of Boghazkoy in modern Turkey) we know a good deal about the Hittites and their beliefs. They were an aggressive, warlike people: their cities were noted for their skilfully constructed fortifications and, appropriately, their primary deity was the powerful god of storms. The Hittites believed it was the business of humankind to serve the gods, who would protect or punish according to how well or badly such service was performed. At the centre of religious and political life stood the Great King, servant-in-chief to the gods and responsible for mediating between Heaven and Earth to placate their anger.

The impressive military strength of the Hittites is shown in this 9th-century BC relief, depicting a triumphant king in one of the battle chariots for which they were renowned.

They were not a notably artistic people – no Hittite work can compare with the Babylonian statuary at Ur or Uruk – and their literature was mainly borrowed from the neighbouring populations, although the unique, varied mythology of Anatolia is quite different to that of Mesopotamia. Locally derived tales were usually closely linked to religious observance, their recital often forming part of important ceremonies.

However, it was as a military power that the Hittites made their presence felt in the region, reducing nearby kingdoms to vassal status and making forays further afield. In 1595BC, a Hittite army led by one King Mursilis got as far as Babylon itself – a rich target for looters. The Hittite occupation of the city ended the dynasty which was established centuries before by Hammurabi. But Mursilis's hold on Babylon was brief and, laden with the riches of plunder, he soon returned to Hattusas, where the volatile dynastic politics required his active intervention.

In fact, a single empire extending all the way from the western coast of Anatolia to the Mesopotamian plain was simply too large to be managed. Revolts and internal power struggles were frequent. The Hittites seem to have done better in later years, when they relinquished attempts to control the Anatolian coast and abandoned the eastern territory once claimed as their own.

If the Hittites had a golden age, it was probably in the fourteenth century BC when, under King Suppiluliumas, they took northern Syria from the Egyptians and forced much of the area, including Ugarit, into vassalage. They were great ironworkers, and their heavy, three-man chariots were much feared by their enemies.

This period, and that of the successors to this empire, is unusually well documented too, with references in Egyptian archives to Hittite depredations, and a possible appearance in the Hebrew Bible. But these provided virtually the only evidence for the existence of the Hittites until the famous excavation of Hattusas.

The Hittite tradition of decorating buildings with carved stone panels was continued by the Neo-Hittites. This detail from the city of Carchemish shows King Suhis hunting lions.

Despite their military might, the Hittites were swept away by the great population movements of the thirteenth century BC. It was a time of enormous confusion everywhere, when empires were overthrown and mighty cities burned. And it is at this period that the historical record becomes blurred and the fates of entire civilizations obscure.

There are huge gaps in our knowledge of this epoch, and there is no guarantee they will ever be filled. Nevertheless, in one or other of the thousands of unexcavated Near Eastern mounds, future archaeologists may yet unearth missing details – or something still more exciting.

This is not necessarily a fanciful hope. The unearthing of the Syrian city of Ebla in the 1970s, for example, brought to light a vast cuneiform archive that recorded the history of a mighty city-state whose existence had previously been scarcely suspected. There is no reason why Ebla should be the only such city.

After all, this great cultural flowering of the Near East was not temporary, but endured for thousands of years. From the Sumerian invention of writing by 3500BC to its final collapse in the early Christian era Mesopotamian civilization flourished despite a series of invasions. If such an epic story could all but vanish from memory, there may well be whole chapters still unopened, waiting for the attention of an awed posterity.

THE ASSYRIANS

The Assyrians originated from northern Mesopotamia and founded an independent state in the 14th century BC. After a period of rapid expansion and then stagnation in the 9th and 8th centuries BC, a series of strong kings united most of the Middle East. They and their armies spread from the area around Ashur and Nineveh to which they had become confined and, in a little over 200 years, their empire stretched across the fertile crescent and along the Mediterranean coast. As testimony to their influence in Mesopotamia they left a vast artistic and cultural legacy. The magnificence of their architecture and skilled craftsmanship of their art reflected their political power.

Left: **Ashur, the chief Assyrian god, was linked with Enlil, father of the Mesopotamian gods. This 9th-century BC winged disk may represent him.**

Below: **A hunting scene from Sargon II's palace. This splendid palace was decorated with 2.6km of such stone reliefs depicting the life of royalty.**

Above: **One of Assyria's great empire-builders, Sargon II (721–705BC), built a vast palace for himself, 24km northeast of Nineveh. The king's new home had over 200 rooms and 30 courtyards, and was linked by a viaduct to a nearby temple where he had to perform various rites. This carving from the palace shows cedar trunks being unloaded during its construction.**

Left: An enamelled terracotta plaque of the 8th century BC from Nineveh, depicting two merchants. By the early 7th century Nineveh had developed from an important provincial city to become the capital of a growing empire.

Above: This stone carving of *c.*865BC from Nimrud depicts typical activities needed to support an army under the leadership of a martial king like Ashurnasirpal II (883–859BC). The bottom left quadrant shows priests examining an animal's entrails for the purpose of divination, while the other sections show the preparation of food.

A DIVINE REALM

The Mesopotamian gods originated either as elemental forces or as the personification of towns and cities. But they were also portrayed as beings with a full range of emotions and individual characteristics. Like humans, who were ultimately descended from them, the gods suffered from family problems and generational conflict.

The senior gods were headed by An (Sumerian for "sky", in Akkadian called Anu), a somewhat remote authority figure in control of kingship and the cosmic laws that determined individual destinies. A more complex god was Enlil (Ellil), a powerful and aggressive warrior who manifested himself in violent storms, but also prompted and fostered the growth of crops.

Ninhursaga, the primary goddess, represented motherhood and was known in both Sumerian and Akkadian cultures by many other names – such as Ninmah and Mami – according to her different functions. She featured as a midwife in myths of the creation of humanity, in which she often worked in partnership or rivalry with Enki, the craftsman of the gods, who solved problems not with a warrior's force but with cleverness and cunning. Enki used his intelligence to bring the clay in Ninmah's hands to life, just as he fertilized agricultural land by filling the irrigation canals with water, which in Sumerian was denoted by the same word for semen.

The myths about these gods are full of divine battles which can be interpreted as representing the tension between the herding and cultivating economies or the succession of rainy and dry seasons. But the stories also present a range of deities with human characteristics prone to the gamut of earthly emotions. It is not surprising that the gods have mortal qualities, since the life force in humans was thought to be derived from the blood of a deity. Humankind was created to perform heavy labour on behalf of its makers, who regarded them as their progeny, protecting and punishing them by turns.

The society of gods was no different to that of humans, and many of the myths contain an obvious political subtext. Repeatedly they give a divine justification for the institutions of kingship and the temple, crucial to the organization of Mesopotamian culture.

Above: **This Sumerian clay tablet, dating from *c.*3100BC, is incised with signs recording details of agrarian practices which were overseen by the god Ninurta throughout the year.**

Opposite: **Inana, the Mesopotamian goddess who presided over war and fertility, appears both fearsome and seductive in this terracotta relief (*c.*2000–1700BC).**

The most complete and best known Mesopotamian creation myth is the Akkadian story named after its opening words, *Enuma elish*, "When on high ... ". Predominantly a work of propaganda promoting the god Marduk and his city of Babylon, the myth charts the development of the cosmos as if it were a political organization.

This statue of Marduk, great god of Babylon, dates from the second millennium BC. He was mighty in every way: he had exceptional powers of hearing and sight, and he breathed fire.

The *Enuma elish* may date from as early as 1900BC, but was probably composed in its present form around 1100BC to celebrate the triumphal return of the statue of Marduk to Babylon after its humiliating capture by the Assyrians, who held it for a century. The poem was recited each spring on the evening of the fourth day of the Akitu ceremony during the New Year festival.

According to the *Enuma elish,* when the skies above and the Earth below were unformed, only the primordial fresh waters – the god Apsu – and the salt waters – the goddess Tiamat – were in existence. These two waters came together and Tiamat gave birth to Lahmu and Lahamu. The world gradually took shape: Lahmu and Lahamu also coupled and produced Anshar and Kishar, the rims of the sky and the Earth which meet at the horizon. Anshar begat Anu, the Heavens, and Anu begat Ea (known in Sumeria as Enki), the cunning god who would later usurp Apsu and become the god of fresh water.

As the world became more complicated, these beings became progressively less passive and more active. Eventually tension and conflict arose between the inert ancient gods and the restless, striving younger gods, who were endowed with human qualities.

The young gods started to play and shout and disturb the tranquillity of Apsu and Tiamat, so Apsu proposed to exterminate them in order to re-establish silence. Tiamat responded angrily and shouted at her consort, "How could we allow what we ourselves created to perish?" Disregarding her protest, Apsu secretly plotted to kill the younger gods. But Ea, already displaying his nature as the cleverest of the deities, foiled his father: while his siblings panicked he recited a spell which sent Apsu into a deep sleep. Then he seized Apsu's crown and cloak of fiery rays and killed his father.

Having vanquished Apsu, Ea gained control of the deep underground ocean of fresh water which was likewise called the *apsu*. On top of this he established his own temple and dwelt there with his consort Damkina. Here they engendered the handsome and mighty Marduk, who was more splendid than any of his predecessors; he had four eyes and four ears which endowed him with exceptional powers of sight and hearing.

The Mesopotamian Cosmos

In the Sumerian imagination the universe consisted of* an *(Heaven) and* ki *(Earth), the latter envisaged as a rectangular field with four corners. Originally these were fused and inhabited by the gods alone, but at some stage they were separated, possibly to accommodate humankind. All around this universe, both above and below, was a boundless salt-water ocean.

Throughout ancient Mesopotamia, Heaven and Earth were thought to have been formed by means of a cataclysm which churned up the primordial ocean. According to the Babylonian poem, *Enuma elish*, it was Marduk who accomplished this by splitting open the body of the ocean goddess Tiamat (see pages 24–26). In another Sumerian tradition the goddess of the primordial ocean, called Nammu, spontaneously engendered a male sky and a female Earth. At first these two were inseparably joined, until they were parted by their own son Enlil, who then created animals, plants and humans.

But the *Enuma elish* also reveals elements of another widespread view that the cosmos contained several layers: the realm of Anu constituted an upper heaven, the realm of Enlil formed a lower heaven with the Earth beneath, and finally, below that, was the abyss or fresh-water ocean called *apsu*. Other versions of a layered cosmos put the realm of Anu on top, the realm of the Igigi gods (the Sumerian sky gods) below that, and the realm of the stars beneath, closest to Earth.

In addition, there was often said to be an Underworld where the dead were thought to dwell, albeit in inferior conditions. This realm was reached by two flights of steps at the eastern and western horizons. It was thought that the sun passed through gates guarding the Underworld each day as it rose and set, even though it was described as residing in the "interior" of Heaven overnight. The gates to the Underworld were securely barred; and, once inside, there was normally no return (see pages 40–43 and 46–47).

The Underworld was also said to be reached across a river sometimes referred to by the names of actual rivers beyond the furthest boundaries of Sumer. Thus the realm of the dead may have been conceived as some remote place on Earth.

A 7th-century clay tablet from Sippar shows a map of the world and the ocean surrounding it.

Marduk's grandfather Anu made the four winds as toys for the young god to play with. But their games raised storms on the surface of Tiamat, the sea, and disturbed the peace of the other gods. In their annoyance they began to taunt Tiamat for failing to avenge the death of her husband Apsu. Stung by their criticism, the goddess agreed to destroy the young Marduk. She created eleven dragons and other fearsome monsters and put them under the command of the god Qingu to whom she gave the Tablet of Destinies, which bestowed supreme power on its holder.

The First King

At the news of Tiamat's preparations, the gods panicked once again. As before, Ea made the first attempt to subdue Tiamat, but retired defeated. Then Anu tried, but retreated at the mere sight of the raging goddess, who was much more fearsome than Apsu had ever been. Finally the gods begged Ea's mighty son Marduk to save them.

Marduk agreed to fight Tiamat, but on condition that he was given absolute authority over his fellow gods. The younger gods gathered at a celebratory feast and, relaxed by drinking beer, readily agreed to Marduk's conditions. Thus the institution of kingship was established at a moment of emergency for the sake of collective security. Marduk was invested with the king's magical power of command: as the other gods told him, "From this day onward no one will go against your orders."

Decorated with the insignia of kingship and possessed of a fearsome arsenal of weapons, Marduk advanced to fight the enraged Tiamat. He commanded the four winds, which had provoked Tiamat in the first place, to stir her up even further. While Qingu and Tiamat's other helpers became distracted and confused, Marduk forced the winds in through Tiamat's open mouth, inflating her belly. Then he shot an arrow into her distended body and split it open down the middle. Standing on her corpse, he bound her army with his net and seized the Tablet of Destinies from Qingu. This he fastened to his own breast.

With the defeat of Tiamat and the capture of the Tablet of Destinies, Marduk's takeover of the insignia and powers of kingship had reached completion. Now, having gained the status of both a god and a king, he embarked on an organized programme of action. According to Babylonian writers, the heroic struggle with the ocean goddess Tiamat was the first, essential step in the stages of establishing social order.

The first ever king, Marduk, was a great warrior like the Babylonian king in this limestone relief (*c.*1100BC). To win the insignia of kingship, he battled with Tiamat, the ocean goddess.

Marduk contemplated Tiamat's body to see what he could make from it. He split her into two halves "like a dried fish", and made one half into the sky, and the other into the Earth. To emphasize his legitimacy as successor to Ea, Marduk built his own home, Esharra, in the heavens directly above his father Ea's dwelling on top of the *apsu*.

Turning his attention to the heavens, Marduk then established the constellations, instructed the

The Gods of Dunnu

In order to create and dominate the world, the gods resorted to incest and patricide, according to the* Enuma elish*. These motifs recur in other Mesopotamian creation myths, as well as in Hittite and Greek mythology, and they appear regularly in a Mesopotamian myth that explains the origin of the gods. A minor city called Dunnu provides a backdrop to this dramatic story.

In the beginning, there was the Plough and the Earth; from their union they created the Sea. Soon after, the Cattle God and the eternal city of Dunnu came into being. The Cattle God then made love to his mother the Earth, killed his father the Plough and married his sister the Sea. The same pattern was repeated in the following generation: the Cattle God's son, the God of Flocks, likewise killed his father and married his mother the Sea. For generation after generation a series of male gods, some of them named after the flocks and herds which roamed the land, killed their fathers and married their sisters or mothers, who often represented features of the landscape such as a river, tree or meadow.

Although many details remain obscure, the story can be interpreted as representing the changes of the seasons during the year, each one "killing" or replacing the previous one. Eventually, however, the pattern altered dramatically: one of the gods, instead of killing his father so that he could take over his dominion and marry his mother, merely imprisoned him. This happened at New Year, celebrated by the Babylonians during April, which might suggest that this song was recited at the New Year festival. But because the rest of the text is missing, the significance of this interruption in the cycle of patricides has been obscured.

This myth reinforces the general impression given by the *Enuma elish* that creation stories were often highly politicized and they served to glorify a particular city by giving it a pivotal role in the story. In this version of creation, as each god is killed he is laid to rest in Dunnu, a city that was dearly loved by each dead god. As in the *Enuma elish*, the birth of the world is closely linked to the establishment of the most important social and political institution of all – the city.

The Cattle God kills his father, personified as a plough, so that he can couple with his mother. Later, he married his sister, the Sea.

A detail of a glazed mural, which decorated the gates surrounding the inner city of Babylon (*c.*604–561BC), depicts a hybrid creature or monster. Marduk transformed Tiamat's eleven monsters, created to do battle against him, into statues that decorated the temple over the primordial ocean.

moon in its monthly cycle, and made rainclouds from Tiamat's spittle. Next, he formed the Earth from the lower half of Tiamat's body. Then he made the rivers Tigris and Euphrates flow from her eyes and turned her breasts into mountains from which freshwater springs cascaded. As a memorial to his battle with her, he created statues from the corpses of Tiamat's eleven monsters and placed them at the entrance of Ea's temple.

The gods were delighted with Marduk's changes and willingly re-affirmed his title as king. Whereas they had originally conferred this title in an emergency, now they acknowledged his ability to bestow the benefits of stable government. Marduk commanded the gods to build a city which would be both a palace and a temple. This city was to be named Babylon. He also decided to make a new creature. "Let me put blood together, and make bones too," he declared. "Let me make a primeval savage, and call him Lullu, 'Man'. Let him bear the drudgery of the gods, so that they can relax at their leisure." So Marduk asked the assembled gods to name the one who had led Tiamat's revolt. They singled out the prisoner Qingu and he was punished by having his veins slit open. From Qingu's blood, following Marduk's ingenious instructions which were said to be beyond earthly understanding, Ea created humankind.

The creative phase of the story ends there, but the poem continues at length to praise Marduk and to strengthen his link with the city of Babylon and its institutions. Despite the creation of man to dig irrigation ditches, the gods finished the task of building the palace and temple of Babylon with their own hands. At the great feast which followed, they heaped praise upon the weapons with which Marduk had vanquished Tiamat and recited his fifty names, each of which described some aspect of Marduk's character, exploits or cult.

Enki, Creator of the World Order

The* Enuma elish *explains how natural phenomena and social institutions on Earth came to be created and regulated. In an earlier Sumerian source, however, the story is different – everything is established by the god Enki, the clever craftsman who presided over life-giving fresh water. The god's praise is sung both by the author of the poem and in the voice of Enki himself as he celebrates his own might. The goddess Inana also makes a bid for power in the poem (see pages 36–38).

Enki blessed the cities of Nippur, "the place where the gods are born", Ur, Meluhha (in the Indus Valley) and Dilmun (probably Bahrain, see page 28) with abundant crops, flocks, precious metals and success in war. Then he organized the sea, rivers, clouds and rain, turning the barren hills into fields and creating the rivers Tigris and Euphrates by filling their beds with a stream of his own semen. He made the sheep, cattle and crops multiply, and established the skills of building and weaving.

As Enki created each domain, he appointed a god to supervise it. But when he had finished, Inana came to him complaining that he had failed to give her a domain. She described the realms of Nintu the womb-goddess, Nidaba the goddess of surveying, and Nanshe the goddess of the fisheries, and asked plaintively, "As for me, the holy Inana, what is my domain?"

Enki responded by listing the numerous powers and dominions which Inana did indeed have, adding each time, "Young Inana, what more could we add for you?" Unfortunately these lines are fragmented and very hard to interpret, but it has been suggested that he reminded her of her dominion not only of the shepherd's crook and staff, but of the bloody business of battle, and certain kinds of cloth and musical instruments that were linked to war, death and funeral rites as well. Enki concluded that Inana's domain was substantial and extremely powerful, and he finally told her, "Inana, you have the power to destroy what cannot be destroyed, and to set up what cannot be set up."

Enki marshalls all the waters of the Earth and turns the barren hills into fields, before creating rivers and cattle.

Enki and the Island of Dilmun

Enki was able to nurture living creatures and plants with life-giving fresh water (associated with his semen). This gift made him a useful ally for other gods and humans alike. His virility is central to a myth set on the once barren island of Dilmun, which some scholars identify as modern Bahrain.

Enki (centre, right), the cunning god who provided the Earth with fresh water, participates in a New Year ritual. From an Akkadian cylinder seal impression, *c*.2400–2200BC.

Enki slept with the patron goddess of Dilmun, an island described as lacking almost everything – people, animals and fresh water were all absent. So Enki formed a plan: he asked the sun god Utu to make footprints on the ground, so that he could fill them with fresh water transported underground all the way from Ur. The water made agriculture possible and Dilmun became a great centre of foreign trade in luxury goods such as precious stones, rare woods and copper gongs.

In a series of incestuous unions, Enki fathered a number of gods and goddesses. In the first stage of his creation he begged the goddess Ninhursaga to let him sleep with her. She agreed to his request and he poured his semen into her womb so that she conceived. Within nine days of this union she had given birth to the goddess Ninsar.

Ninsar grew up and, as her mother had done, visited the river bank. Enki looked up at her from his domain in the water and desired to possess her. He asked his minister Isimu who was always at his side, "Shall I not kiss this beautiful young girl called Ninsar?" With the encouragement of Isimu, Enki kissed Ninsar and poured his semen into her womb, and once again, after only nine days Ninsar gave birth to a daughter, this time called Ninkurra, Mistress of the Mountains. In the same way, when she came of age, Enki impregnated Ninkurra. After her came another daughter Ninimma, Lady Vulva. She too had intercourse with Enki.

Ninimma in her turn gave birth to Uttu, considered even more beautiful than any woman from the previous generations. Uttu's great-grandmother Ninhursaga warned her not to yield to Enki's advances unless he brought her the fruits of irrigated gardening such as cucumbers, apples and grapes. When Uttu did as she was told and resisted Enki, the god hastened to a gardener whose work had been frustrated by drought. Enki filled up the nearby irrigation canals and in gratitude the gardener gave him the fruits he needed.

When Enki presented the gifts to Uttu she let him make love to her. As he poured his semen on to her body, she cried out, and, in a passage which is hard to decipher, it seems that Ninhursaga heard the cry and rushed to her great-granddaughter's aid. She quickly wiped Enki's semen from Uttu's body and planted it in the ground nearby.

This time, instead of creating a daughter, Enki's semen sprouted into eight different kinds of plant. Now when Enki looked up from the river he saw not a beautiful girl, but these unusual new crops. Since he did not realize that they were his own offspring, and fuelled by his curiosity, Enki asked his minister Isimu to harvest these oddities for him so that he could discover their nature. Isimu did as he was told, and gave the plants to his master who decided to eat them.

Enki grew sick and, for reasons which the text does not make clear, Ninhursaga swore that she would no longer be associated with him. The other gods sat down in the dust in despair, until a clever fox, carefully dressed for the occasion, managed to persuade the goddess to return. She had sex with Enki whose illness had spread to specific parts of his body. Ninhursaga was able to cure him by giving birth to eight deities whose names corresponded to his afflicted body parts. Among the eight deities were the lords of Dilmun and Magan (Oman in Arabia).

Thus the myth resolves the horror of repeated incestuous rape and the constant threat of Enki's unbridled desire and sexuality. With the assistance of the benign mother Ninhursaga, however, Enki is saved from severe illness, and eight deities, favourable to humankind, are born.

Vital Water

Enki's domain was the apsu, an ocean of fresh water which was believed to lie deep beneath the ground. It was vital to existence on Earth.

Civilization in Mesopotamia depended on an elaborate and extensive systems of canals created to irrigate the land between the Tigris and the Euphrates. Regular spring floods washed away the boundaries of fields and necessitated the development of a more sophisticated system of surveying. To dig and maintain these canals required a centralized authority to organize and control mass labour.

The development of kingship, law and writing was thus closely linked to the regulation of the water supply, which was policed by a special canal inspectorate. It was said that whoever controlled the canals controlled the land, and cities often went to war over access to water.

Verdure cloaks the Island of Ana in the river Euphrates, a source of water for Mesopotamian civilizations.

The Suffering of Humanity

Creation was seen as an act of skilled craftsmanship. In this myth, Enki the chief craftsman is challenged to a creature-making contest by Ninmah (another name for Ninhursaga, the mother goddess). As a result of Ninmah's inadequate skills, a number of tragic defects were introduced to the world from which humanity continues to suffer. The entire text is a hymn of praise to Enki and concludes with the words, "Ninmah could not rival the great lord Enki. O Father Enki, your praise is sweet!"

In the old days, the gods were forced to work hard excavating irrigation canals. The senior gods did the digging while the younger gods carried away baskets of earth. They all complained bitterly about their circumstances. But the only god able to alter their fate was the wise and resourceful Enki, and he was deep in sleep in his watery domain. So Nammu, the mother of all the gods, went in search of him and roused him so that he might fashion a substitute to undertake the arduous task. Enki, "the creator of forms", was deep in thought for a while and then said to Nammu, "Mother, you yourself can knead such a thing from the clay which lies above the *apsu*. Let the goddess Ninmah assist you." And so it came about, while Nammu decreed the fate of each human being, Ninmah's task was simply to command the individual, after creation, to carry baskets of earth.

The figures incised on this alabaster vase of the Uruk Period (*c.*4000–3000BC) found in modern-day Iraq present offerings to the gods, who created the world.

After the task had been completed, Enki held a feast to celebrate the new-found leisure of the gods, who praised him for his accomplishment, saying, "Oh lord of wide understanding, who is wise like you? Who can equal your actions?" As the feast progressed, Enki and Ninmah overindulged and drank too much beer so that they became intoxicated. Belligerently, Ninmah said to Enki, "I could make humans by myself and give them a good or bad fate, as I please." Enki replied, "Whatever kind of human you create, I can turn to advantage the fate you bestow on it."

Ninmah set about making her first human. Perhaps deliberately to challenge Enki, perhaps because she had only been Nammu's assistant and had limited skill, she produced creatures with serious physical defects. Yet despite their handicaps, Enki was able to find a useful role for each of them. When Ninmah made a man unable to stretch out his hands and grasp things, Enki made him a servant of the king because he would not be able to steal. The second man she made was blind, but Enki gave him the gift of musicianship so that he too could serve the king. Translators have not

A detail from the Standard of Ur (*c.*2600–2400BC), which once decorated a royal cemetery, depicts court servants and musicians. Their roles are explained in the creation myth featuring Enki and Ninmah.

been able to decipher the nature of Ninmah's third creature, but her fourth was a man who could not hold his semen. Enki was able to cure him by giving him a purifying bath. Ninmah's fifth creature was a barren woman, but Enki turned this to her advantage by placing her in a harem. The sixth and final creature, a sexless being, was also appointed as an attendant to the king. Enki concluded "I have found a role and given bread to every misformed creature of yours."

Having outdone Ninmah, Enki had to challenge her in turn, and it seems that he deliberately procured unfortunate beings in order to test her abilities. His first creature was a woman who was having difficulty in giving birth. Ninmah's powers proved insufficient to reverse her fate. His second being was an *umul*, or very old man whose heart, bowels and lungs were so afflicted that he could not answer Ninmah's questions. Frustrated, Ninmah complained that he was neither alive nor dead – she could do nothing to improve his deteriorating condition.

While Enki had managed to provide Ninmah's malformed individuals with positive roles that were recognized within the community, Ninmah proved unable to do the same for Enki's creations, so their disabilities remained a problem for Mesopotamian society. The vagaries of creation had come into being as a result of Enki's drunken gambling with the ambitious Ninmah.

A Journey to Nippur

The story of the construction and blessing of Enki's luxurious and magical temple at Eridu is contained within a hymn of praise to the god himself. To ensure that the temple was fully consecrated by the other gods, Enki had to journey by barge to Nippur, around a hundred kilometres to the north, where he entertained them at a lavish feast.

The ruins of Eridu, dating back to the Ubaid Period, lie in the desert land of southern Iraq. In ancient times the city was a centre for the worship of Enki.

The temple, decorated with silver, lapis lazuli, cornelian and gold, was established on the bank of a river, where its foundations reached deep into the underground waters of the *apsu*. It had magical qualities: the brickwork gave Enki advice, while the surrounding reed fences roared like a bull. The roof-beam was shaped like the bull of Heaven, and a lion gripping a man formed the gateway. The overall effect was described as a lusty bull.

The bustle of activity there was compared to the drama of a river rising during a flood. Enki had filled the building with lyres, drums and every other kind of musical instrument. Surrounding the temple was a delightful garden full of fruit trees, with birds singing all around and frolicking carp playing among the reeds in the streams.

Enki called up the beat of the *ala* and *ub* drums and set out by barge to Nippur in order to receive the other gods' blessings. The fish danced before him in the waves and the river Euphrates swelled as it would before the south wind. The sound of the water around his barge was like the mooing of a good cow, and Enki had slaughtered numerous oxen and sheep for the feast to come.

Once disembarked at Nippur, Enki entered a shrine and began preparing beer in great bronze vessels. Then he set out a feast for his father Enlil and the other gods. Paying attention to protocol, he seated An at the head of the group with Enlil beside him and the goddess Nintu in a seat of honour nearby. In the feasting which followed, the gods consumed great amounts of the beer. Enlil was extremely happy and in front of all the Anuna gods pronounced his blessing on Enki's new temple: "My son Enki has made his temple ... grow from the ground like a mountain."

A Bountiful Harvest

Several poems describe a god's journey or procession by barge. They probably relate to rituals in which statues of gods were ferried from their home cities to a site of pilgrimage where they received a blessing. In Eridu, the poems were usually sung as praise to the god Enki, as keeper of the* me *(cosmic laws), and in Nippur to Enlil, as chief of the gods.

In the spring time, a barge bearing the year's first yield of dairy produce would set out from the city of Ur. At the city of Nippur the goods would be exchanged for produce made by the herders of the south around Ur and those of cultivators in the north around Nippur.

The patron god of Ur was the moon god Nanna (also called Suen or Sin). In a mythical version of this ritual, Nanna decided to visit his parents Enlil and Ninlil at Nippur. He sent men to all the corners of the Earth to gather materials for building a barge and rejoiced as they returned one by one with precious cargos of exotic woods. Nanna then prepared a rich array of gifts for his parents and set off on his journey.

On the way upstream, Nanna stopped at five different cities. At each stop, the patron goddess of the city, seeing his abundant cargo, would welcome him and press him to stay, but at each stop he refused, saying, "I am going on to Nippur."

Finally, the barge docked at the quayside in Nippur and Nanna announced the full list of his offerings to his father's doorkeeper, who was delighted and opened the gates to the temple. Enlil was similarly overjoyed by his son's arrival and staged a banquet, offering him his best beer. In return for his herders' gifts, Nanna asked Enlil for a blessing and some produce from the local fields. Enlil gave him all that he asked for and in great joy Nanna took these blessings home to Ur.

The moon god Nanna ferries a rich cargo of gifts to present to his parents, Enlil and Ninlil, at Nippur.

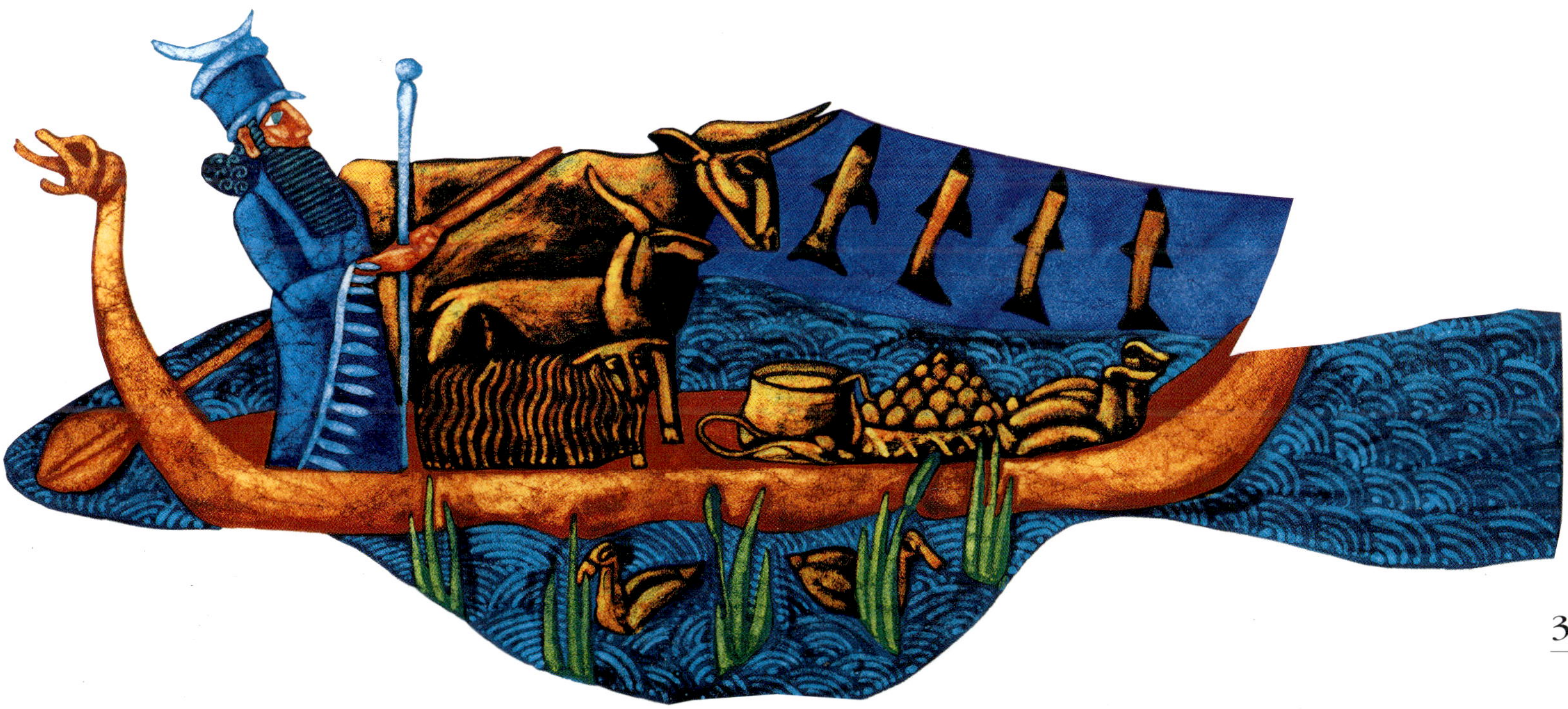

How the Moon was Saved

In one myth Enlil, as the god of spring rainstorms, married the goddess of the young corn, Ninlil ("Lady of the Wind"). Together they produced a son Suen (Sin or Nanna-Suen), the moon, known as "the Bright Lone Divine Traveller". But unfortunately, once born, the moon was destined to stay in the Underworld forever; unless his parents could think of a way to appease the Underworld gods. Luckily, his father Enlil came up with a cunning solution that allowed his son to travel through the sky at night.

The first encounter between Enlil and Ninlil is reminiscent of the story of Enki and Uttu (see pages 30–31). Ninlil's mother warned her young daughter not to bathe in the Nunbirdu canal because Enlil might seduce her and make her pregnant. But Ninlil disobeyed, and Enlil, delighted by the sight of her naked body, did indeed proposition her from the opposite bank. For a while Ninlil refused him, saying that she was too young, her lips were unused to kissing and that her parents would be angry. She also argued that she would find it difficult to keep the romance secret from her girlfriend.

Unwilling to accept her rejection, Enlil ordered his servant to make him a boat so that he could cross the river and join her. By the time he reached the opposite bank, Ninlil had already changed her mind and agreed willingly to his advances. The couple made love and she became pregnant with the moon god Suen.

But when Enlil returned to Nippur, he was arrested, falsely accused of raping Ninlil. Branded a sex offender by the fifty great gods and the seven decision-makers, he was banished from the city. To fulfil his sentence, Enlil had to go on a long journey which took him as far as the river leading into the Underworld.

So Ninlil, who did not want to be separated from her beloved, set out in pursuit. As he passed out through the city gate, Enlil said to the keeper of the gate, "Ninlil is following close behind me. If she asks you where I have gone, do not tell her."

Substitutes for the Moon

When Ninlil reached the gate and asked the gatekeeper about Enlil's whereabouts, the gatekeeper replied, "I have never had the privilege of chatting with Enlil." Ninlil proudly told him that

A Babylonian boundary stone from the Kassite Period (*c.*1415–1154BC) depicts King Melishipak II presenting his daughter to the moon god Suen, son of Enlil.

In Praise of Enlil

In eulogies to Enlil his great powers in the realms of agriculture, fertility and civil organization were praised.

Enlil encouraged humans, cattle, fish and crops to multiply. The text which recounts the story of his relationship with Ninlil ends: "You are the lord! You are a great lord, a lord of the granary! You are the lord who makes the barley sprout! You are the lord who makes the vines sprout!"

Enlil's managerial role extended to the sanctioning of social institutions. Another hymn to him proclaims: "Without Enlil's warrant, no city could be built and settled, no cattle-pen or sheepfold could be constructed, no king or lord appointed, no high priest or priestess picked out by a divine sign."

As the god of fresh water, Enlil's favour had to be won by all farmers to ensure a good harvest. This farmer, depicted on an Akkadian cylinder seal (*c.*2200BC), uses a plough drawn by an ox.

Enlil had made her pregnant and that she was carrying the precious moon in her womb.

Somehow, the gatekeeper knew that the unborn moon had to be saved from an eternity stuck in the Underworld and offered to impregnate the goddess with another child, saying, "May the sperm which will become the moon go heavenward, and may my own progeny go to the Underworld as his substitute."

Ninlil agreed and lay with the man in the gatekeeper's chamber. Little did she know that Enlil had disguised himself and exchanged places with the gatekeeper. In this way, she conceived a second son by Enlil called Nergal, who was indeed destined to remain in the Underworld forever and reign there as king (see pages 46–47).

Enlil continued on his journey, and again Ninlil followed close behind. Eventually he reached the mountain river that led to the down into the Underworld. As before, he told the guardian of the river not to reveal to Ninlil where he had gone. Not long afterwards, Ninlil arrived at the river. She asked its guardian where Enlil was and received the same reply as before. Again, she announced that she was bearing the moon in her womb and the guardian offered to impregnate her with a second substitute who would also remain down in the Underworld.

Again, the man she lay with was Enlil in disguise, and she conceived the Underworld god called Ninazu. At the third and final stopping point in the journey, Enlil disguised himself again. Ninlil, thinking that she was coupling with the ferryman of the Underworld, conceived Enbilulu, who became a god of the Underworld river. In this way the Moon was saved for the upper world by the creation of three substitutes.

Lady of Heaven

Inana is the most complex of all the Mesopotamian goddesses. Her name is Sumerian and probably means "Lady of Heaven". Her Akkadian name, Ishtar, is related to that of the Syrian goddess Astarte. Inana was variously called the daughter of An, Enlil or even Enki. In the myths of her lover Dumuzi's death (see pages 42–44) she is the daughter of the moon god Suen (Nanna) and sister of the sun god Utu. Her elder sister is Ereshkigal, queen of the Underworld, and an intense jealousy rages between the two of them.

Inana's principal shrine was in the great city of Uruk, although it is likely that local goddesses in other places were also assimilated into her cult over time. This may explain why Inana combines several different roles which seem incompatible. As Lady of Heaven, Inana was identified with the planet Venus, whose disappearance and reappearance in the night sky may be reflected in the myth of her descent to the Underworld and her return (see pages 40–43).

Inana is also sometimes portrayed as keeper of the cosmic laws, or *me*, which, according to one myth, she obtained from her father Enki while he was drunk (see opposite). Her constant quest for greater powers led her to try to take control of her sister's realm of the dead. This lust for power may have complemented her role as a goddess of war, in which she is described as enjoying battle as if it were a game or a dance. She is portrayed in Mesopotamian art as a heavily armed warrior.

Yet Inana is perhaps best known as the goddess of amorous liaisons and sexual love. In the Epic of Gilgamesh (see pages 74–93), Inana is reproached for her maltreatment of a series of lovers, and the hero himself turns her down. More tragically, her passionate affair with the shepherd god Dumuzi ends with his death and the goddess's grief.

Inana was also the protectress of prostitutes. One of her most important jobs in this aspect was to couple once a year with the real-life king. This union may have been performed ritually by the living king with a temple prostitute, who stood in for the goddess.

The combination of all these aspects creates a fully rounded character who is headstrong, ruthless, and dangerously seductive to men. Whether she appears as a virgin or as sexually promiscuous, Inana is always portrayed as a young woman free of the usual responsibilities of a wife and a mother.

A relief from Tell Asmar shows Ishtar (Inana), standing on her sacred lion. This 8th-century BC Babylonian artefact depicts the goddess as a powerful warrior.

The *Me*

The* me *(pronounced "may") were the unwritten fundamental laws of the universe. They formed the basis of society and ensured that the cosmos could function.

The most comprehensive surviving list of *me* gives around one hundred powers, not all of which are easily translated. These constituted offices and roles such as kingship, priestship, godship, eldership, and occupations including scribe, shepherd, blacksmith and leatherworker. Others included important human actions, qualities of character, moral values and emotions. Law, music and art feature, as do enmity, judgement, wisdom, truth, falsehood, sexual intercourse, prostitution, the destruction of cities, lamentation and rejoicing.

These properties were considered to be the basic components of action and consciousness that dictate human existence. Some were thought to reside in material objects such as drums which contained rhythm, or thrones which embodied kingship.

To possess the *me* was immensely empowering but also entailed great responsibility. Generally they were said to be conferred by the senior male gods An or Enlil, but in one tradition they were handed over to Enki for safekeeping in his temple at Eridu. They could also be transferred from one god to another if a task had to be delegated. Like the Tablet of Destinies (see page 49) they could be stolen.

Inana, who on one occasion complained that she did not have enough power (see page 27), contrived to take the *me* from her father Enki, who resided at Eridu, to her own patron city, Uruk. Inana visited Enki, who received her with hospitality and generous amounts of beer. As they sat together drinking, Enki became more and more intoxicated and offered the *me* to Inana, instructing his minister to hand them over to her one by one. When she had gathered them all, Inana loaded them onto her barge and cast off for Uruk.

The effect of the beer wore off and Enki realized that the *me* were missing. He questioned his minister, who told him that he himself had just given them all away. In consternation, Enki sent his official in pursuit of Inana to demand their return.

Six times his minister caught up with the goddess at halting points on her route home, and each time various creatures from Enki's subaquatic realm challenged her and tried to regain the *me*. First, a little frog was despatched, then other animals followed in its wake. Unperturbed, Inana pointed out that Enki had given her the powers under oath. Finally, having kept her cargo intact, the goddess reached her own city of Uruk in triumph and unloaded the *me*.

The title of scribe is one of many offices incorporated in the Sumerian *me*. On this neo-Hittite stele, the scribe Tahunpigas is represented as a child on his mother's knee.

The Rape of Inana

Shu-kale-tuda was a mere gardener's boy who dared to rape Inana – presented in this myth in her role as custodian of the *me*, or cosmic laws. The story suggests that in violating the goddess, Shu-kale-tuda also violated the *me*, putting his whole nation under threat from the wrath of the goddess.

One day Inana ascended the mountains so that she could view the land of Sumer, to search out falsehood and injustice and distinguish criminals from righteous people. This process is described as "allowing the *me* to display their perfection".

Eventually, wearied by her inspection of Heaven and Earth, the goddess lay down to rest in the deep shade of a poplar tree. She carried the *me* in the form of seven holy tablets which she had tied tightly across her lap. Catching sight of her from his vegetable garden nearby, Shu-kale-tuda approached Inana and lay down beside her. He then removed the tablets and raped her while she was asleep. Before dawn, he returned with the tablets to the garden.

Inana awoke, realized what had happened and determined to find the culprit wherever he might be hiding. But, in her anger, she also punished the land of Sumer three times over. First, she turned the water in all the wells into blood and the people could find nothing that they could drink. Shu-kale-tuda understood from this sign that he was in trouble and confessed his crime to his father, who advised him to join his brothers in the city, where he would escape detection among the crowd. Although Inana searched for him high and low, she failed to find him, so she punished Sumer once more, this time with floods and dust storms. Shu-kale-tuda continued to avoid detection by hiding in the city. Her anger mounting, Inana punished the land for a third time, in a way which cannot be deciphered in the text, but once again, the guilty Shu-kale-tuda evaded her.

Finally, Inana turned to her father Enki at Eridu for help. Somehow, Enki was able to help her isolate Shu-kale-tuda from the crowd, rendering him small and helpless. Cornered at last, the malefactor confessed his guilt and Inana pronounced judgement on him. "You must die," she said, "but, nevertheless, your name will live on in a song which will be sung throughout the land, from the king's glorious palace to the remotest and humblest shepherd's camp."

The goddess Inana sleeps with the holy tablets of the *me*, or cosmic laws, strapped across her lap. But they will not protect her from the amorous advances of a gardener's boy.

The Goddess and the Bandit Woman

There are several versions of the myth of the death of Inana's lover, the shepherd Dumuzi. In this story, rather than handing him over to his murderers, Inana takes vengeance on the old bandit woman Bilulu and her son, who killed him in order to steal his herd. Like many poems about Dumuzi, the story opens with a lamentation for his demise.

When Inana learnt that Dumuzi was dead she burst out weeping at the loss of her lover. "Dumuzi, with your fair mouth and kind eyes! Oh, my boy, my husband, my provider, sweet as the date!"

Summoning courage, she asked her mother's permission to go to the sheepfold where he had been horribly killed. As she approached the fateful spot, she remembered the terrible details of how Dumuzi had been found with his head badly beaten. She was even further incensed at the thought of his sheep and cattle being herded away by the bandits who had stolen them.

Again, Inana sang a lament, praising Dumuzi's tireless work. As she sang, she felt her heart swell with a great desire to avenge her lover. And so, while the old bandit woman Bilulu and her gang were counting their ill-gotten gains, Inana determined to kill them so that her beloved could rest in peace.

She discovered them in a beer-house, stole up to them and ruthlessly killed them. To make the punishment fit the crime, she also cursed Bilulu and transformed her into a waterskin so that shepherds like Dumuzi could use her to quench their thirst in the desert heat. "Let the old woman gladden his heart!" she declared grimly. She also transformed Bilulu's son into a desert spirit who job would be to call Dumuzi to receive libations of water and flour whenever humans placed and poured these offerings upon the ground. In this way Dumuzi's spirit was returned to the desert, "the place from which he had vanished".

Unlike some other versions of Dumuzi's death, there is no mention in this story of his subsequent resurrection each year, although his presence in the desert to receive offerings could be interpreted as such. This version concludes with Inana joining his sister Geshtin-ana. Together the young women lamented the death of the young man that they had both loved.

A ritual bowl (*c.*300BC) from Uruk is decorated with domesticated grazing animals. Inana's lover, Dumuzi, was the deity of shepherds and, in one myth, he died at the hands of marauding bandits. His spirit was thought to reside in the desert.

A Descent into the Underworld

An early Sumerian version of this myth depicts proud Inana's impulsive and assertive character to the full as she ventures to the Underworld only to be unexpectedly humbled by her elder sister Ereshkigal. Like the story of the descent of Nergal to the Underworld (see pages 46–47), which has survived in two versions (both written in Akkadian), this story confirms that no one can return from the netherworld without cost.

One day, the goddess Inana decided to descend to the Underworld. She dressed confidently in all her finery and took with her the seven tablets of the *me*. But as a precaution she left instructions with her maidservant Ninshubur: "If I do not return within three days, you are to beat the funeral drum and cry a lament for my death. Go to Enlil for help. If Enlil will not help, go to Nanna. If Nanna will not help, go to Enki, the one who knows the herbs and water that bring the dead back to life."

Having left these instructions, Inana set out and was soon hammering at the gates of the underworld to be given entry. When Ereshkigal's minister Namtar enquired of her business, she made the excuse that she had come for the funeral of her sister's husband Gugalana. Namtar passed her message on to Ereshkigal, who was greatly disturbed. Biting her lip, she told him, "Let her in, but mind you bolt each of the seven gates tightly as she passes along the road of no return."

As Inana proceeded through each of the first six gates, she was gradually stripped of her items of jewellery from the upper world. She was shocked by this, but Namtar told her that this was in accordance with the *me* of the Underworld which were different to those of Earth. At the seventh and last gate, her dress was removed and Inana stood naked before Ereshkigal.

Ereshkigal descended from her throne and Inana rushed forward and sat there in her place. Her impetuous attempt at seizing power, however,

Inana was forced gradually to remove all her ornaments as she passed through the seven gates of the Underworld. This beautiful necklace from Sumer dates from *c.*2600–2400BC.

The demon Pazuzu was commonly depicted with a canine face and scaled body. Although he was regarded as an Underworld monster, women wore representations of him on chains around their necks to protect their children from death.

was short-lived. The seven judges of the Underworld looked upon her with the perishing stare of death and she was turned into a corpse and hung on a hook.

Meanwhile, in the upper world, Inana's servant Ninshubur prepared to carry out her instructions. She journeyed to Enlil's temple in Nippur to plead with him to rescue her mistress, but the great god flew into a rage, shouting, "Inana was not satisfied with dominion in the upper world but craved power in the lower world too! Having accepted the *me* of the Underworld, she must remain there!"

Unperturbed, Ninshubur then went to the temple of Nanna in Ur, but here also she was denied help. Finally, she made her way to Enki's temple in Eridu. Enki complained that he was tired of Inana's foolish escapades, but nevertheless agreed to rescue her. He scraped some dirt from his fingernails and created two sexless creatures who were able to enter the Underworld and return with impunity. Enki gave them the life-giving plant and restorative water, and specific instructions for their journey: "Steal into the Underworld, passing like flies through the gaps by the hinges of the gates. There you will find Ereshkigal in labour. As she cries out in pain you must echo her cries. She will appreciate your sympathy and will offer you anything you wish as a reward. But even if she offers you a whole river to drink and a field of corn to eat, you must not accept them. Ask only for the corpse of Inana."

The sexless creatures carried out their instructions with precision and everything happened as Enki had predicted: Inana's corpse was revived with the life-giving plant and water, and the three of them set off back to the upper world. It seemed that Enki's plan was succeeding, but just before the refugees reached safety, the seven judges of the Underworld caught up with Inana and seized her, saying, "Who has ever risen from the Underworld alive?" They insisted that if she was to escape, she must provide a substitute to take her place in the realm of death. To ensure that she did so, they sent an escort of demon guards *(galla)* to accompany her to the land of the living.

The first person that they met on Earth was Ninshubur herself, clothed in rags of mourning and thrashing in the dust. Inana could not bring herself to condemn her faithful servant to a life in the Underworld, and so they went on to seek another substitute. They met Shara, the god of the city of Umma, who was also in mourning. Inana was unwilling to consign him to death, as he was her singer, hairdresser and manicurist.

Then, under the great apple tree in the plain of Kulaba, they came upon Inana's lover, the shepherd god Dumuzi. But far from mourning for Inana, Dumuzi was sitting on a magnificent throne, clothed in glorious raiment. Inana was incensed and agreed to his capture. As the demons seized him and spilled the milk from his churns on to the

Demons of Death

Some Mesopotamian demons were created by the gods as weapons of war, but the* galla *demons of the Underworld (humorously named after real-life law-court officials similar to modern-day constables) were sent to arrest those destined to die.

The pitiless nature of the *gallas* is emphasized by their lack of normal human needs and emotions. They did not enjoy food or drink, nor did they indulge in the pleasure of sexual intercourse, and they never experienced the joy of playing with children. Instead, they snatched children from their parents' knees, and stole young brides from their marriage chambers.

In the account of the shepherd Dumuzi's death in which he dreams of his own demise (see page 44), the *gallas* relentlessly pursued their quarry.

In some ways they resembled hunters, and it is perhaps significant that in another version of Dumuzi's death, he takes the form of a gazelle. But the way in which they destroyed Dumuzi's camp and knocked over his milk churns suggests that the *gallas* were also modelled on the bandits who presented a real threat to Mesopotamian society.

Some demons had beneficial powers: the winged monster in this 9th-century BC Assyrian relief is gripping a symbol of purification.

ground, Inana looked upon him with the very same look of death to which she had been subjected by the seven judges of the Underworld.

Dumuzi turned pale and appealed to Inana's brother, the sun god Utu, to transform him into a snake so that he could wriggle out of the demons' grasp. It seems that Utu answered Dumuzi's prayer. The metamorphosis, however, lasted only half the year. It also seems that Inana regretted handing Dumuzi over to the demons, and agreed that his sister Geshtin-ana should remain in the Underworld for half the year, as his substitute.

Ishtar and her Sister

In the shorter, Akkadian, version of this story, Inana is called Ishtar. As in the earlier Sumerian version, her motive for descending to the Underworld seems to have been a wilful desire to take over her sister's realm. Her behaviour at the gate was similarly aggressive, and she added a chilling threat: "If you do not open the gate I shall smash it down and release the dead into the upper world, so that they outnumber the living!" This version describes Ereshkigal's fear of her younger sister: "Her face grew livid as cut tamarisk, her lips grew dark as the rim of a black-lipped cooking vessel." The text also makes it clear that Ereshkigal was tricked against her will into handing over her sister to the rescuers from the upper world.

As in the Sumerian version, Ishtar passed through each of the seven gates and was progressively stripped, until finally at the seventh gate her dress itself was removed. Once again, she was told by the gatekeeper that this was the custom of the Underworld. Ereshkigal then sent sixty diseases to attack her sister's naked body and hung her on a hook, not as a corpse, but as a waterskin.

Meanwhile back on Earth, preparations were being made to orchestrate Ishtar's rescue. In this version the gods were forced to act by a curse of sterility which fell upon the world of the living. Without Ishtar's presence, procreation ceased among both animals and humans. In this version too, it is Ea who contrived her rescue: he created a pretty young man and sent him down to Ereshkigal's realm to lighten her mood. He succeeded and when the time came to name his reward, he asked for the waterskin which represented the remains of Ishtar. When she heard this, Ereshkigal said, "You have asked me for something that you should not have!" She cursed the young man to a life of poverty and squalor, but nonetheless was forced to release Ishtar who returned through each of the seven gates, with her belongings restored to her.

There is no mention in this story of the seven judges and their guards, nor of Dumuzi's transformation into a snake. Instead, the role of Dumuzi as a substitute is not debated, and instructions are given for his funeral rites. It is possible that these instructions related to an annual ritual which was held at Nineveh in the month named after Dumuzi, part July and part August, during which a statue of the shepherd was laid out for burial. Dumuzi's sister Belili (equivalent to Geshtin-ana) lamented his death, and declared that Dumuzi's return from his half-yearly stay in the Underworld would be the occasion for a burial rite.

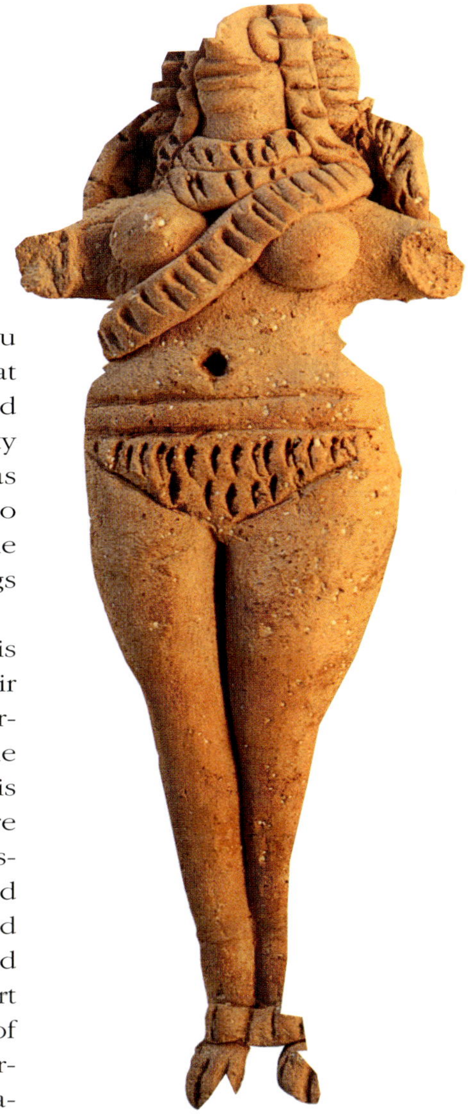

During her passage through the seven gates of the Underworld, Ishtar was requested to remove her jewellery and clothing. This Akkadian figurine from the Agade Period (*c.*2400BC) shows her with a minimum of clothing.

Dumuzi's Dream

Another myth tells an alternative version of the shepherd god Dumuzi's death. Instead of being killed as a substitute for the goddess Inana, he is ruthlessly hunted down by *galla* demons after having a dream that predicts his own end. Perhaps the moral of the story is simply that death is inescapable.

A modern-day scene depicting marshlands near the river Euphrates. In such a place, the shepherd god Dumuzi dreamed of his own death.

The shepherd Dumuzi went out on to the plain, "his heart full of tears" and called the marsh and its creatures to lament for him. Overcome by foreboding, he lay down to sleep, and dreamed a terrifying dream which he later recounted to his devoted sister Geshtin-ana, who was able to interpret dreams. She explained it to him: "It is clear that your dream is not auspicious! It foretells your death."

Dumuzi begged his sister to go up on to a mound and look out for the *gallas*. He gave her advice on how to act: "Scratch your body and tear your clothes as a sign of mourning, to let them think I am already dead." Geshtin-ana did so and swore that she would never betray him.

The *gallas* caught Geshtin-ana and tried to persuade her to betray her brother's whereabouts, but she refused their bribes of a river of water and a field full of corn. The demons gave up, saying, "Ever since the world began, who ever saw a sister betraying her brother's hiding place?" So they then offered the same bribe to a friend of Dumuzi's, who readily revealed the shepherd's location and the *gallas* quickly tracked him down.

Dumuzi appealed to his brother-in-law, the sun god Utu to help him elude his captors by transforming him into a gazelle. Utu answered his prayer and Dumuzi bounded off. But the *gallas* soon caught up with him. Once more Dumuzi appealed to Utu, who helped him escape to the house of a trustworthy old woman called Belili. But Belili could not conceal that she had a visitor. The *gallas* burst into her home so that they could capture him again. In desperation Dumuzi fled toward his own sheepfold. When Geshtin-ana saw him coming, she immediately set up a cry of lament and scratched her body in mourning to confound the *gallas*. But the demons realized from her behaviour that something was amiss. Suspecting that she was hiding her brother, they burst into the sheepfold. There, they overturned his milk churn, tore his drinking mug down from its peg, and killed Dumuzi. Events had come to pass exactly as his dream had foretold.

Nomads and Farmers

As a deity who died and was resurrected in a seasonal cycle, Dumuzi was sometimes associated with the growth and harvest of corn and fruit. He is, however, more firmly linked with the herding and breeding of domesticated sheep and cattle, which required a nomadic lifestyle.

While the growth of crops is dependent on groundwater and moist winds, breeding sheep and cattle relies explicitly on the act of mating. The cult of Dumuzi was dominated by sexual ritual. The story of his liaison with Inana provided a model for kings who would engage in symbolic sexual union with the goddess. This ceremony was intended to ensure the fertility of the land.

In one text Dumuzi argues from the viewpoint of a pastoralist in a dispute with Enki, the god of irrigated agriculture. Their economies were seen as complementary, and herders and cultivators would sometimes exchange produce, as shown in the story of Nanna-Suen's barge journey to Nippur (page 33).

But relations between farmers and nomadic herders were sometimes tense and at times even hostile. Occasionally conflict could arise. Settled peoples regarded nomadic tribes as wild and primitive and were fearful of their raids.

Despite a long history of resistance to nomadic peoples – a wall was built in 2034BC in an attempt to keep them out of northern Mesopotamian cities – the nomads continued to travel across the land and sometimes won for themselves positions of power, even becoming kings. An important nomadic people of the western desert was the Martu, known in the Bible as the Amorites. One myth tells how the king of the agricultural city of Aktab wished to reward the god of this tribe, himself called Martu, for a heroic deed that he had performed. The king offered him a substantial amount of silver and lapis lazuli, but Martu had no use for such valuables. All he wanted was the hand of the king's daughter. She was happy with this proposal, and so was her father.

The daughter's companion, however, tried to dissuade the princess from marrying a nomad by painting a harsh picture of the barbarous way of life that she would be forced to endure if she joined Martu.

The woman criticized him: "He lives in a tent exposed to the wind and the rain. He does not know how to pray, and he eats wild truffles. He is insubordinate and shows no respect for authority, and he eats raw meat. He does not possess a house while he is alive, and after death he has no burial."

A shepherd clasps a lamb to his chest in this 3rd-millennium terracotta statuette.

The Marriage of Nergal and Ereshkigal

The two myths that tell how Nergal came to rule with Ereshkigal are filled with violence and eroticism. In the earlier version, from the fifteenth or fourteenth century BC, Nergal visits the Underworld, seizes Ereshkigal's throne, and remains there as king. In the seventh-century BC version, Nergal escapes to the upper world but cannot exist without his queen.

The gods in Heaven were feasting, but their sister Ereshkigal could not come up from the Underworld to join them, so they invited her to send her minister Namtar (whose name in Sumerian means "Fate") to collect some delicacies from the table. When Namtar arrived, all the gods knelt before him out of respect for the goddess of death, with the exception of Nergal. Namtar returned and reported the news to Ereshkigal, who was furious. "Bring Nergal to me," she said, "and he shall die!"

Namtar approached the gods with Ereshkigal's demand, and they agreed that Nergal should be taken captive because of his irreverence. But Nergal hid among the other gods and, although he tried, Namtar was unable to find him. So the minister returned alone to Ereshkigal, who sent him again to find the offender. No longer able to hide, Nergal appealed to his father Ea, who responded by giving him seven pairs of demons to assist him in the Underworld.

No sooner had Namtar admitted him through the outer gate of the Underworld, than Nergal's fourteen demons pushed through and stationed themselves in pairs at each of the seven gates leading into Erishkigal's domain. This allowed Nergal to rush through the gates unhindered into the goddess's palace. There he seized her by the hair and pulled her from her throne, intending to cut off her head. But Ereshkigal begged him to be her husband: "You will be master and I shall be mistress!" At these words, Nergal wept, then brushed away his tears and kissed her.

Nergal met the goddess of death, Ereshkigal, with the help of fourteen demons. Pazuzu, a wind demon, is depicted in this 7th-century BC Assyrian statuette.

Ea suggested that Nergal should take an imitation throne with him to the Underworld. It might have resembled the chair in this banquet scene from the walls of the Southwest Palace at Nineveh (*c.*630–620BC).

In the later version, Nergal sleeps with Ereshkigal on his first visit and then escapes, but cannot resist returning. In this version, Nergal made the journey to the Underworld because death, personified as Ereshkigal, fascinated him. But since he wished to return to the upper world again, his father Ea made him build a wooden chair to take with him. This chair was an imitation throne, painted and set with coloured pastes to simulate silver, gold and lapis lazuli. This may refer to part of a Babylonian funeral rite in which a chair was left out for ghosts to sit on, to distract them and prevent them from seizing a living person.

Ea instructed Nergal not to sit in any other chair while in the Underworld, nor to accept any food, or sexual relations with Ereshkigal, as all these would make it impossible for him to return.

But Nergal caught a glimpse of Ereshkigal naked after bathing. Initially he resisted the temptation to seduce her, but eventually he gave in and they embraced passionately. After they had made love for seven days, Nergal escaped, and Ereshkigal fell into a fit of grief. She sent Namtar back to the gods to beg them to return her lover to her.

As in the earlier version, Namtar was unable to locate Nergal – Ea had disguised him as an idiot. But then Nergal apparently decided to return to the Underworld of his own accord. On his arrival, Namtar gave him some advice. "Beware of the keepers of the seven gates who will try to catch you as you pass through." Nergal knocked down each of the gatekeepers before they could catch him, and rushed to join Ereshkigal. With a laugh he seized her by the hair and pulled her from her throne. They embraced and then made love again for another seven days, and it was decreed that Nergal should stay with Ereshkigal forever.

The Warrior King

Enki's son Ninurta was the god of the thunderstorm, the flood and the plough, and an impressive warrior. The most important myth about him comes from *Lugale*, a poem which has these opening words, "Oh Warrior King!" The myth tells of how Ninurta fought a mighty monster in the eastern mountains and conquered its family of rocks that had rolled on to the plains to attack civilization.

As Ninurta was feasting with the other gods, he received some bad news from Sharur – his loyal weapon, the mace whose name meant "Smasher of Thousands". It was able to move around independently and communicate with the gods. High up in the mountains, the rocks and plants had risen in revolt against the plains, Shamar told Ninurta. As their leader they had chosen a fierce warrior called the Azag. The Azag did not have human qualities: it was a kind of stone, resistant to the blows of the spear and the axe. To spread its progeny far around the land, the Azag had intercourse with the mountains. Incited by the Azag, rocks constantly were rolling down the mountains to crush cities on the plain. Sharur warned Ninurta that the Azag was taking control of the eastern border districts and was plotting to snatch away his kingship.

A detail from a 3rd-millennium BC mosaic shows a warrior guarding a prisoner. The motif of battle and civil unrest is woven into the myth of the Azag monster to explain the occurrence of natural phenomena such as landslides.

This report spoiled the atmosphere of the feast and sent the gods into a panic. So Ninurta, dressed and prepared for war. Then he set out in all his glory, heralded by tempests of wind and fire, to confront his enemy. The Azag had flattened hills and destroyed all the forests in his path, pinioned birds to the ground, boiled the fish in the rivers and crushed the population of the rebel region as if they were butterflies.

Sharur, having gone ahead to reconnoitre, came back with a warning. Despite the great monsters that Ninurta had conquered in the past, he would be no match for the Azag, who was unlike any other opponent. But Ninurta took no notice of Sharur's advice and pursued his attack.

In the mighty battle that ensued, the Azag attacked Ninurta with massive landslides. It flung a wall of rock against him, tore up tamarisk trees by the roots and gouged gashes in the Earth. Ninurta began to retreat. An, Enlil and the other gods were dismayed, but the mace Sharur flew off to Ninurta's father Enlil for advice, and returned with a message. "Your father says you should keep attacking the Azag with your rainstorm and eventually you will be able to thrust your spear into it." With this encouragement, Ninurta finally overcame the Azag. He also cunningly destroyed its power to reproduce itself, thus ensuring a complete end to its tyranny.

Ninurta Civilizes the Rocks

Ninurta's victory over the leader of the mountain army thus assured, he began to adapt the wild

Ninurta and the Turtle

A fragment of a text in Sumerian contains an amusing episode from a longer story about the theft of the Tablet of Destinies by the formidable Anzu bird. In this version the custodian of the Tablet is the god of fresh water, Enki. The story pokes fun at Ninurta, who is taught a lesson in humility by Enki who enlists the help of a turtle.

After Anzu had stolen the Tablet and flown off with it, Ninurta attacked the bird and made him drop the Tablet back into the *apsu*, Enki's watery domain. Enki was delighted and praised Ninurta as the great conqueror of Anzu, saying that his name would be honoured for ever.

But Ninurta was not satisfied with this blessing. His face went dark and pale in turns, and he started to plot against Enki. He decided that he wanted to take over the whole universe, and the key to this plan lay with the Tablet of Destinies. But Enki, being clever, guessed what was in Ninurta's heart. As a warning he stirred up the waves of his *apsu* and sent his minister Isimud to see his son. But Ninurta's arrogance was so great that he even dared to raise his hand against Isimud.

After his conflict with Enki, Ninurta finds himself trapped in the nest of a giant turtle that was created in order to torment him by his own father, Enki.

This was too much for Enki. In exasperation, he moulded some clay from the *apsu* to form a turtle. Giving it life, he set it to work scraping out a deep pit with its strong claws. When Ninurta continued to threaten him, Enki retreated gradually towards the trap. Suddenly, the turtle came out from behind him and seized Ninurta, while Enki gave him a shove into the pit.

Ninurta was unable to climb out of the hole. Enki stood on the edge of the pit and looked down at Ninurta far below, where he was still being clawed by the turtle. "You were planning to kill me," he mocked loudly, "you with your big ideas! You have tamed mountains and now you can't even climb out of a pit dug by a turtle! What kind of a hero are you?"

Fortunately for Ninurta, his mother Ninhursaga came along and saw her husband tormenting their son. She stopped to reprimand Enki and reminded him of the time she saved his life when he had eaten the eight plants (see pages 28–29). "What about you, you plant-eater?", she demanded, "I saved you, so now save your son!"

mountain rocks for use by humankind. The myth recounts that in those days the mountain streams did not flow down into the plain; instead their waters ran uncontrolled and were wasted. The art of digging and dredging ditches was at that time unknown to human society, so Ninurta decided to improve the situation by using the rocks which he had conquered. He piled them up to create embankments for watercourses and to channel the flow into a river so that the mountain waters could be used to sustain the barley in the fields and the fruits and vegetables of the orchards and gardens. This long and hard campaign kept Ninurta away from his home. His mother Ninmah had been missing him and complained that he had neglected her during his conflict with the fierce Azag. So Ninurta proved his affection for her by giving her a brand new name in honour of his organization of the rocks into channels that guided the waters down the mountains to the plains. He called her Ninhursaga, "Mistress of the Rocky Foothills".

Ninurta embarked next on the second stage of his plan to use the rocks advantageously. He analyzed each kind of rock and decided on a function for it. This section of the story gives an explanation for the technological use of a wide range of important minerals imported from the mountains into Mesopotamian cities. Each use is presented as either honourable or humiliating, according to Ninurta's decision either to reward or to punish that particular type of rock for its conduct in the mountain revolt.

Not all of the rocks referred to in this myth can be identified, and some of the processes associated with them are hard to envisage. Some rocks he punished by making them vulnerable to erosion; others were forced to become grinding powders used to break down the other rocks; others were carved, pierced and polished in various ways. He punished lava and basalt, which had formed ramparts against him, by making them into moulds for goldsmiths. Limestone, which had plotted to seize Ninurta's office, was designated for use in foundations on muddy ground; it was also destined to crumble rapidly in water. Flint was punished by having to flake at the touch of an animal's horn. However, those rocks that had changed their allegiances during the battle and refrained from assaulting Ninurta, the storm god decided to reward. For example, dolerite Ninurta chose to turn into an enormous statue in the E-ninnu temple in Girsu. It was decreed that lapis lazuli and other precious stones that had not committed offences should also be honoured.

Having conquered the rebellious rocks, Ninurta gave them functions such as providing material for artists. This statuette of Ebih-Il, an official at the Temple of Ishtar, in Mari (*c.*2400BC), is made of alabaster.

The Creation of Humankind

The creation of the world is presented in the *Enuma elish* as a primal, elemental process which heralded the social charter of kingship established by the god Marduk (see pages 22–27). The story of Atra-hasis, however, is concerned primarily with the creation of humanity and its early history. A human figure rather than a god emerges as the central character. Atra-hasis, whose name means "Extremely Wise" in Akkadian, also appears in the Epic of Gilgamesh, where he is called Ut-napishti, "He Who Found Life".

The Flood was perceived as an historical event by the ancient Mesopotamians. The Sumerian King List is divided into those who ruled before and those who ruled after the Flood (antediluvian and postdiluvian). One version of this list describes Atra-hasis as king of the city of Shuruppag.

Atra-hasis is clearly a precursor to the biblical Noah. Like Noah, he was chosen to survive a deluge intended to destroy humanity and was warned to build a ship and fill it with pairs of animals. But in contrast to Noah who was under orders from the one God of the Hebrews, Atra-hasis was at the whim of a quarrelling pantheon.

Before the creation of human beings, when the gods did all the work, dominion over the cosmos was divided by lot. The realm of the sky was allocated to Anu, the Earth to Enlil and the ocean to Enki. These senior gods, called the *Anunnakku*, forced the junior gods, the *Igigi*, to dig the Tigris, the Euphrates and numerous irrigation canals.

For 3600 years the *Igigi* tolerated this imposition. But eventually they rebelled, burning their tools in a demonstration staged outside the house of Enlil, god of the Earth on which they toiled.

Enlil was frightened at the anger of his own descendants and his face turned as sallow as tamarisk wood. He summoned his fellow rulers Anu and Enki for a conference and asked the strikers for the name of their leader. But the *Igigi* replied, "Together we have declared war on you! Our work is too hard, it is killing us!" Enlil continued to try to single out the strikers' ringleader, but Anu and Enki pointed out that the demonstrators were not altogether wrong: "Why are we complaining? Their work really has been too hard."

The once marshy banks of the river Euphrates have been transformed into pasture land by irrigation. Before the creation of humankind, it was the task of the junior Mesopotamian gods to dig the canals for drainage.

Anu and Enki suggested that a substitute should be created to relieve the junior gods. They asked the womb-goddess Mami (also known as Nintu and Belet-ili) to make a new kind of creature. Enki, the clever craftsman, explained what to do. "Select one of the junior gods and kill him. Then let Nintu mix clay with his blood and his intelligence. God and man will be mixed together in the clay and we shall hear the drumbeat forever." The beat of the drum may have represented the sound of the tem-

As humans were created from the blood of a sacrificed god, ancient worshippers made libations to their creators through sacrificial offerings. A mural from 18th-century BC Mari, in northern Mesopotamia, shows a priest leading a bull to its death as an offering.

ple drum when it was played by humans worshipping the gods, or possibly the sound of the human heartbeat.

Mami and Enki went into a secret place where they moulded humans, seven female and seven male, out of fourteen pieces of clay, in a process which was clearly based on the processes of brick-making. A rebel *Igigu* god was selected for sacrifice, so although human life contained a divine portion, it was also inherently flawed because it came from a recalcitrant god.

Humanity Proliferates

The gods' act of creation gave rise to trouble. Six hundred years later humans had become a pest on the surface of the Earth; they were "as noisy as a bellowing bull". Angered, Enlil declared, "I can't sleep for the din. Order an outbreak of plague."

Just as in the *Enuma elish* Apsu had tried to kill the noisy younger gods, so Enlil now decided to take action. He first made three attempts at long intervals to reduce the human population, and it was only when these did not work that he finally decided to send a devastating flood which would wipe them out altogether. At each of these attempts, Enlil's plans were frustrated by the special protective relationship which the god Enki had formed with a loyal human called Atra-hasis.

In his first attempt, Enlil told the plague god Namtara to kill large numbers of humans. But sympathetic Enki taught Atra-hasis and his people to ignore the other gods and to sacrifice only to the god Namtara, as the source of their distress. The god was flattered by their unaccustomed attention and decided at once to bring the plague to an end.

However, after another 600 years, humanity had once again become too numerous and noisy. So Enlil instructed the rain god Adad to withhold his rain and cause a drought on Earth. But again Enki taught humans to sacrifice directly to Adad, who, feeling flattered, secretly moistened the Earth with dew at night and mist in the morning, so that the harvests could survive.

Some time later, Enlil mounted his next attack on humanity. This time he arranged for Heaven, Earth and water to conspire so that every means of nourishment was withheld from the people. For six years the rivers failed to rise, salt crystals appeared on the surface of the parched fields and women's wombs became constricted so they were unable to give birth. Year after year, the people grew more desperate until by the fifth year they were selling their own children, and by the sixth year they were killing and eating them.

At this point the text fragments and it is not clear how total extinction was averted. But once again it was the initiative of Enki that returned water to the Earth.

Enlil was furious and summoned an assembly of the gods. He berated them for sabotaging his plan and persuaded them to collaborate in another scheme that would finally rid the Earth of humanity. He intended to send a flood that would wipe out everything in existence.

Suspecting that Enki, loyal as ever, would warn humanity to save itself, Enlil forbade him to communicate with the people on Earth at any time. But Enki found a way to circumvent Enlil's prohibition: he addressed his warning to a wall of reeds, knowing that Atra-hasis was lying awake behind it, trying to decipher a recent dream. Time was short and Enki spoke tersely. "Listen very carefully," he said. "Destroy a house and build a boat. Abandon your property and save life. Roof the boat all over and seal it with strong pitch."

Atra-hasis understood the mes-

The exultant rain and weather god, Adad, stands astride a steer on this 800BC basalt stele from Assyria. He caused a drought that almost wiped out humankind.

sage and set his people to work building a boat. He was so nervous that "his heart was breaking and he was vomiting bile", but he continued to gather up pairs of every kind of creature, from wild animals to birds. He only just managed to seal the door and cut the mooring rope when the rain god Adad began to bellow from the gathering storm clouds. The ensuing tempest drowned the remainder of humanity "like dragonflies". The womb goddess Mami who had created the human race watched the raging waves and heard her offspring screaming for help. She wept to think how she had complied with Enlil's wicked plan.

The flood lasted for seven days, and as it continued the gods began to suffer terrible hunger cramps caused by the lack of sacrificial offerings from humankind. When Atra-hasis's boat finally ran aground, his first action was to make sacrifice to the gods, who gathered around the delicious aroma like flies.

The only exception was Enlil, who surveyed the failure of his grandest plan and asked angrily, "How

Some of the animals that Atra-hasis probably took on to his giant boat are depicted in this detail from the exquisitely crafted Standard of Ur (*c*.2600–2400BC). The rest of the scene is a victory feast.

did any man escape this catastrophe?" Enki confessed that he had secretly prepared Atra-hasis for the deluge by suggesting that he build a boat. But he agreed to work with the womb goddess Mami in devising other ways of controlling the human population.

To this end Enki and Mami created three kinds of being who would help reduce the birthrate. The first was a class of infertile women, the second a demon who would steal and kill young children, while the third consisted of several kinds of religious devotee for whom it was prohibited to bear children. In this way the myth presents a lack of fertility in some humans as a compensation for excessive fertility in others.

The Entry to Heaven

In a number of myths the boundaries between the mortal and divine worlds are crossed. The story of Adapa, like that of Gilgamesh (see pages 74–93), explores the impossibility of attaining immortality, while the tale of Etana describes the difficulties of accomplishing a successful mission to Heaven.

Like Adapa the man in this fragment of a frieze from Sennacherib's palace, Nineveh, is a fisherman. The water god, Ea, played an elaborate trick on Adapa and he lost an opportunity to attain immortality.

Adapa was the first of seven sages who lived before the flood. Despite his wisdom, he was unable to avoid being tricked by the god Ea. And in the process he missed an opportunity of becoming immortal himself and releasing the human race from inevitable death.

Adapa was a priest and a fisherman. One day he was caught in a violent storm and his boat was sunk by the south wind, so he cursed the wind and "broke its wing". After seven days the god Anu noticed that the south wind had ceased to blow, so he asked his minister to tell him why. The minister replied that Adapa had cursed it. Anu immediately sent for Adapa so he could explain himself.

Before setting off, Adapa received two pieces of so-called advice from Ea, the god of water, whose real intent was to deceive him. First, he told Adapa how to pass through the gates of Heaven into Anu's presence and make Anu well disposed towards him. "You must dress in mourning. When you meet the gods Dumuzi (see page 44) and Gizzida who guard the gates, you must tell them that you are mourning the deaths of none other than Dumuzi and Gizzida themselves. This will set the two gods laughing and in their merriment they will appeal on your behalf to Anu. You can accept the oil and the robe he will offer you, but you must on no account accept the bread and water."

On arrival at the gates of Heaven, everything happened just as Ea had predicted. Adapa gained the favour of the two guards so that when Anu berated him for damaging the south wind with his curse, Dumuzi and Gizzida put in a good word on his behalf and Anu was appeased.

The next stage of Ea's deceitful plan then came into play. The god of water had warned Adapa off the bread, using a subtle pun so that his words could be understood as the "bread of death" when actually they meant the "bread of Heaven". Similarly, he had allowed Adapa to interpret the offer of a robe and oil as hospitable, rather than as part of a funeral rite.

Now that the gatekeepers had made Anu well disposed towards Adapa, the god regretted the sorrows that Ea had forced upon humanity and offered Adapa the bread and water of life, along with the robe and oil so that he could throw them away. But Adapa remembered Ea's warning and without understanding their meaning, he put on the robe and anointed himself with the oil of death, as if preparing himself for the end, while refusing the bread and water of eternal life.

Then Anu laughed in amazement at Adapa and asked him, "Why didn't you eat? Why didn't you drink? Didn't you want to be immortal? What a pity for suffering humanity!" Adapa realized his mistake but it was too late. Ea had tricked Adapa into unwittingly rejecting eternal life.

Etana's Journey to Heaven

Etana, king of the city of Kish, was unable to produce a son and heir. Each day he prayed to the sun god Shamash and begged him to point out the plant of birth that restored fertility.

Shamash told Etana to go across the mountain, where he would find an eagle trapped in a pit as a punishment for eating the children of a snake that he had befriended. The god suggested that Etana save the bird of prey. Etana found the eagle and nursed him back to health. The grateful eagle promised to look for the plant of birth. He flew all around the mountains, but without any success. Returning, the bird suggested they fly to Heaven to request an interview with Ishtar, mistress of birth.

Etana seated himself on the eagle's back and they soared upward. After the first league, human affairs on the Earth below seemed no more than the buzz of flies and the sea was no bigger than a sheepfold. At the third league, the land looked like a garden and the sea like a bucket, and at the fifth, neither was visible at all. Losing his nerve Etana, begged the eagle to return him to safety and so he had to endure a dizzying descent.

But then Etana had a dream in which he and the eagle entered the gates of Heaven together. Thus encouraged, he once more set out on the eagle's back. This time he did not panic and eventually he and the great bird flew through the gates of Heaven. The end of the story is missing but it seems likely that Etana's mission was successful since the Sumerian King List records that Etana lived for 1560 years and had a son named Balih who duly succeeded him.

The god Shamash, depicted with a symbol of the sun, sits in majesty before three worshippers. This stone tablet dating from the 9th century BC was made in honour of a Babylonian king who renovated the Temple of Shamash at Sippar.

CREATURES OF THE IMAGINATION

One of the most striking features of Mesopotamian art is its fantastic bestiary. Winged bulls, winged lions, animals with human heads, and other supernatural beings decorate the walls of temples and palaces, and stand guard over their entrances. They have been found in the remains both of some of the earliest cities and in the glorious palaces of the Assyrians. For the people of the ancient Middle East the world was populated by fantastical creatures, but this bizarre menagerie was invisible to ordinary mortals. Magic, therefore, was a necessity of everyday life, to ward off these demonic spirits as well as to counter the effects of wrongful actions.

Right: This beautiful ivory carving of the 8th century BC is only 19cm high and 15cm wide. It depicts a lion with a human face, sometimes known as a sphinx. Such creatures are common in Assyrian art, and could be either male or, as in this case, female.

Left: Two demons, one with an animal head and the other with a human head, dating from the time of the Assyrian king Sennacherib (704–681BC). Demons were semi-divine, and could be either "good" or "bad". Whereas good demons acted independently, so-called "bad" ones were mere instruments of the gods, meting out punishments to wrong-doers. It was unusual for them to be depicted in art before the first millennium BC, when the idea of an Underworld inhabited by evil spirits began to spread through the Middle East.

Right: This lion-headed monster with staring eyes is made of terracotta. Demons were commonly depicted with lion heads. Such objects were protective, intended to drive away less friendly spirits.

Above: Symbols of the gods Nergal (left) and Marduk carved on a Babylonian boundary stone (*c.*1120BC). Nergal, represented by a lion-headed staff, was associated with the Underworld, and described as the husband of Erishkigal, goddess of death.

Below: Bulls were commonly associated with the storm god, Haddad. This stone carving of a winged bull from Syria, dates from the 9th century BC.

Left: Genies, like the winged one in this 8th-century BC carving from Ashur, are often found in Assyrian art. Sometimes they are depicted as half-animal, at other times as minor gods. His horned cap symbolizes divinity.

Above: This 9th-century BC sphinx found in Syria unusually wears the double crown of Upper and Lower Egypt. Although the sphinx is often associated with Egyptian mythology it has Mesopotamian origins.

Above: This baked clay plaque from Babylon of *c.*700BC shows animal intestines configured to resemble the face of the demon Huwawa, who Gilgamesh killed (see pages 80–83). Intestines were consulted for divination.

Below: Figures of bulls with human heads are common on Mesopotamian buildings throughout the ancient period. They are often found on palace walls or guarding gateways. This example is from Girsu, north of Ur.

A LAND OF CHAMPIONS

The earliest versions of the heroic Sumerian tales were probably sung by minstrels at the courts of kings whose own deeds were the source of inspiration for the songs themselves. Those stories that have survived – the earliest written versions date from around 2100BC – all refer to the daring acts of three great rulers of Uruk, kings in the early days of the city's history: Enmerkar, Lugalbanda and Gilgamesh. According to the King Lists (clay tablets recording specific dates and traditions marking the lives of Mesopotamia's monarchs), they lived some time before 2600BC. Their exploits and their destinies were to become the subject of the oldest known literature in the world.

Most cultures have an age of heroes whose legendary feats inspire awe and pride. Sumer was no different – except for the immense antiquity of its origins. Its heroic epoch was staged in the early third millennium BC. During this time the first cities were being established and the conflict between city and wilderness is a recurring theme of the myths.

Although the three lords of Uruk have their roots firmly in history, by the time their adventures were preserved for posterity on baked clay tablets, generations of poets had transfigured their original deeds into larger-than-life legends. Thus Enmerkar was said to have built the first walls of Uruk and single-handedly invented writing. He was a cunning hero – winning his battles as much by ingenuity as by might – and the darling of the gods, especially Inana, Lady of Heaven and protector of Uruk. Lugalbanda, who learned his fighting skills as a captain in Enmerkar's army, was also divinely favoured. Thanks to the intervention of the gods, he survived an ordeal in a mountain wasteland that would have killed any ordinary man.

Lastly came Gilgamesh, the greatest of them all. As a mighty warrior, ruler, lover and demi-god ("one-third human, two-thirds divine"), he features in dozens of the region's most exciting stories. He is described as the first king of Uruk, the city which he built himself, but the bulk of the legend deals with the story of his friendship with the wild man Enkidu and a quest for eternal life. Gilgamesh may appear obsessive and doomed in his determination to evade death and become immortal, but his conviction and fortitude made him the supreme hero of Sumer, Babylon and, in time, of the entire Near East.

Opposite: **The hero in the centre of this Hittite carving has been identified as Gilgamesh, sheltering under a sacred symbol composed of a winged disk supported by a pair of bull-men.**

Above: **A heraldic figure, associated with Enkidu, the companion of Gilgamesh, decorates this gold plaque made in Persia *c.*350BC.**

Enmerkar Outwits the Lord of Aratta

Long ago, during the legendary age of Sumer's past, a great *en*, or priest-king, ruled in Uruk. He was Enmerkar, the earliest of Sumer's trio of superheroes. An epic tale based on his exploits tells how he used cunning in a contest of wits to bend a rival to his will. In the process he brought the blessings and all the advantages of the written word to the ancient land of Sumer.

Snow-capped mountains in Mesopotamia typify the hostile setting against which the ancient cities of Uruk and Aratta fought out their age-long feud.

As the *en* of Uruk, Enmerkar was the ritual husband of the goddess Inana, upon whose favour the city's prosperity depended. In this he was not unique: the goddess shared her favours with the *en* of other cities too – but not equally. Enmerkar was her preferred lover, and he intended to ensure that he remained in favour.

To please the powerful goddess Inana, he planned to build a lavish temple in Uruk, which would stand out against the city's mudbrick dwellings "like silver in a lode". But there was one small difficulty: Enmerkar had none of the precious stones and metals at hand that would be needed to decorate his new shrine.

He knew where he could obtain them. Far from Uruk, "over seven mountains" – which probably places it somewhere in modern-day Iran – lay the city of Aratta. It was common knowledge that its lord had more than enough gold and precious stones to complete Uruk's new temple so that its splendour could be enjoyed by all.

To put pressure on Aratta, Enmerkar used his most powerful weapon: the fickle favours of Inana. As an *en,* the Lord of Aratta also had a particular relationship with the goddess, but she had admitted that she favoured Uruk's master. So when Enmerkar implored her to prevent rain from falling on the distant city until its ruler had yielded the treasure needed for the temple, Inana agreed.

Enmerkar sent an envoy to the drought-ridden Aratta with demands that were backed with threats to destroy the city. At first, despite these threats and the famine that afflicted Aratta, the *en* was defiant. "What does your master's word mean to me," he sneered. "Tell him there will be no bowing down of Aratta to Uruk!" But when the envoy explained that Enmerkar had Inana on his side and that Aratta's growing hardships were the goddess's work, then the lord became so angry that he was unable to speak.

But he was not ready to give up yet. Without Inana's help, he knew he could not hope to defeat Enmerkar, so he proposed a duel of wits, setting his rival three apparently impossible problems. Enmerkar rose to the challenge.

First, he requested grain to ease the famine – but in order to test Enmerkar, he insisted that it be delivered in open nets, not in sacks. His opponent quickly found a solution. Inana was not the only deity on his side, and Nisaba, goddess of grain, revealed to him her divine knowledge. On her advice, Enmerkar sent Aratta malted grain that was so swollen with fermentation that it would not fall through the nets. With the grain he sent a message demanding that Aratta accept, in a well-understood gesture of submission, a sceptre from Uruk. So be it, agreed the rival lord, but only if the sceptre were a unique one. "Let it be not wood," he began, "or called by the name of wood ... Be it not gold, be it not copper ... " and continued with a long list including every material known to him.

Once more, Enmerkar found an answer – thanks to the intervention of Enki, god of the marshes. On his advice he grew a sceptre from a type of reed, the like of which had never been seen before in Sumer. His rival was baffled again.

He issued one last challenge. "Let the matter be decided by single combat between champions from the two cities," he declared. But the Lord of Aratta expected no ordinary warrior from his rival. Enmerkar's champion had to be dressed in colours that were not black, nor white, nor brown, nor green nor any hue at all. This time, Enmerkar found the answer without divine aid: his champion would wear undyed cloth, of no named colour.

The tale, in its surviving form, omits details of the combat itself; presumably Enmerkar's warrior gained the victory. Anyway, despite having won all three rounds of Aratta's duel of wits, the *en* of Uruk was now out of patience. Again he sent his envoy to the distant city, telling him to say to its lord, "May I not have to scatter this city like wild doves from a tree? ... May I not have to appraise its value for the slave market? ... May I not have to scoop up dust as it lies in ruins?"

The list of threats was long and terrifying, and Enmerkar realized that his ambassador might have difficulty remembering them all. So to the astonishment of his court, he set them out in the very first letter the world had ever seen.

As a negotiating tool, the written word proved decisive. The Lord of Aratta gazed with dismay at the clay tablet – "The words were fierce, they were frowning" – and knew he was outclassed. At long last, the precious stones and metals were made available for Enmerkar's temple and the rulers indulged himself in a well-earned song of praise: "They will always say, he was able to bring gold to our city."

The conflict between the cities of Aratta and Uruk was to be decided in a battle of champions such as the one portrayed on this ivory tablet from 7th-century BC Nimrud.

The Contest between Sorcerers

The rivalry between the cities of Uruk and Aratta was ancient and deeply felt. Although, as we have seen, Uruk usually won the day, Aratta continued to fight back. The hero Enmerkar took part in at least one other struggle with his rival – but this time he enlisted the help of a magician rather than relying on his own cunning.

In this tale, for the first time, we are given the name of the Lord of Aratta: En-suhgir-ana. He may have been the man defeated by Enmerkar in the earlier duel of wits, or a successor; either way, he was defeated once again.

The quarrel began when an envoy from En-suhgir-ana arrived in Uruk with an insulting message for the city's ruler: Enmerkar must submit to the Lord of Aratta, for only he was the true bridegroom of Inana. En-suhgir-ana alone, the envoy claimed, would "lie in sweet slumber with her on an adorned bed". Although Enmerkar might see the goddess in a dream, only En-suhgir-ana could meet her face-to-face.

Enmerkar was of course incensed. Was not he himself, of all Sumer's rulers, Inana's favourite? En-suhgir-ana could keep his "adorned bed": Enmerkar would continue to sport on the splendid flower-strewn bed of Inana. After giving a few intimate details of his nights with the goddess, Enmerkar sent the envoy back to his master to convey his contempt. Not only was his sexual performance at stake, his relationship with Inana formed the basis of his power as Uruk's ruler.

Rebuffed, En-suhgir-ana took counsel over his next step. Now there happened to be in Aratta at that time one Urgirnuna, a refugee from the distant, destroyed city of Hamazu. Like others from his lost birthplace, he was a man of great magical powers. On the advice of his chief minister, En-suhgir-ana sent the sorcerer to Uruk to do what harm he could, giving him copious provisions for his journey: "He ordered fine herbs for him to eat, and fine water for him to drink."

En route for Uruk, Urgirnuna stopped off at the city of Eresh on the banks of the Euphrates –

These swamps between the Tigris and the Euphrates appear much as they must have done when the sorcerers Urgirnuna and Sagburru held their battle of wits by the water's edge.

A World Ruled by Magic

Life was good for Mesopotamia's city dwellers – they were, after all, among the first people to enjoy the advantages of an urban existence. But they regarded their prosperity, and even their very lives, as constantly under threat from supernatural influences – whether ill-natured demons, sorcerers, or capricious gods. The well-being of humankind was also at risk from what the Akkadians called* arnu *and the Sumerians* namtaga*, a kind of sickness that afflicted those who might have unknowingly violated taboos.

Despite the advanced technology used to build cities, and the sophisticated institutions developed in order to run them, the city dwellers lived in a world imbued with magic. And the only defence they knew was counter-magic, carefully prescribed incantations and rituals organized by skilled practitioners. These offered some protection in a precarious, haunted environment.

No real distinction was made between magic and medicine, or magic and divination: for everything there was an appropriate spell, usually sanctioned by immemorial tradition. The oldest known spells date from 2400BC, and subsequent evidence attests to the fact that they were still being used more than a thousand years later, acquiring, over the generations, a rich accretion of additional ceremony.

Such rites typically involved a combination of precisely memorized incantations incorporating a host of objects and ingredients such as wool, flour, onions, even sea water, all invested with a symbolic power. Other more exotic ingredients were used: bat's blood and crushed scorpion, for example, were needed to seal gaps around doors in one ritual.

No doubt such magical performances were not without effect. If people believed that their troubles were caused by bewitchment spells no doubt seemed the proper way to solve them.

Of course, really effective magic depended on the availability of a trained magician – a respected practitioner whose services carried a high price. Not everyone could afford such treatment. But amulets inscribed with powerful protective incantations could be worn by everyone.

Sacred amulets, including solar discs, thunderbolts and crescents, confer protective power on this gold and silver Babylonian necklace dating from around 1800BC.

A 7th-century BC relief from Nineveh shows King Ashurbanipal out hunting lions. In ancient times in Mesopotamia the beasts were so numerous and destructive that stalking them was a necessity as well as being a sport enjoyed by royalty.

presumably then a part of Enmerkar's domain – to demonstrate his impressive skills. He entered the cattle-pens and sheepfolds, cursing cows and sheep alike until he caused devastation throughout the land. There was no milk in the udders of the cows; as the text says "the day darkened for the calf". Cowherds and shepherds wandered off in tears, hungry and begging help from the sun god. They had every expectation of receiving it, for Eresh was sacred to the grain goddess Nisaba, known to be friendly with Enmerkar (see page 64).

Help duly arrived in the form of a counter-attack from Sagburru, an old sorceress who appeared at the riverside and began a sequence of contests with the enemy magician. Each round began with the throwing of a *nun*, a copper talisman, into the river, before each sorcerer conjured a creature from its depths. The first time, the sorcerer pulled a plump carp from the charmed waters, but the old woman produced an eagle which seized the fish and flew off with it into the mountains. The second time, he pulled out a ewe and a lamb; the woman matched them with a wolf which dragged the ewe away. For the third encounter, Urgirnuna created a cow and its calf; Sagburru, in turn, created a lion, strong enough to overpower and seize them both. When Urgirnuna took an ibex and a wild sheep from the Euphrates, Sagburru countered with a leopard. And in the final round, the sorcerer's gazelle was viciously destroyed by the old woman's fierce tiger.

Urgirnuna was now. greatly discomfited: "His countenance darkened and his mind became confused." Scornfully, the witch Sagburru berated him. "Sorcerer, you may have magical powers, but where is your sense?" Had he not realized that by harming those under Nisaba's protection, he was challenging the goddess herself?

Uruk Triumphs

In vain, Urgirnuna begged the old woman to spare his life. But pointing to the ruined cattle-pens of the goddess, she told him, "You did a forbidden thing. You made the cream and the milk scarce." So she killed him on the spot and then flung his corpse down into the depths of the vast Euphrates.

This defeat was too much for En-suhgir-ana, who promptly abandoned the demands he had made to Enmerkar. He sent another envoy to Uruk, this time carrying a very different message: "You are the beloved of Inana." The humble En-suhgir-ana, clearly horrified by the death of his sorcerer, went even further in his self-abasement: "From the moment of conception, I was not your equal; you are the big brother. I cannot ever match you."

Once more Enmerkar had triumphed over his rival but this time without even lifting a finger; the cunning sorceress had won the contest on his behalf. Truly, he was the beloved of the gods.

A Monument to Presumption

An ancient tale of linguistic confusion recounted in the book of Genesis may have originated at the time of Enmerkar. The story of the Tower of Babel is a warning against pride: when the first city dwellers erected a tower intended to reach the heavens, the Lord punished their presumption by confounding language, so that they could not understand each other's speech.

The biblical story is thought to date from around 600BC, when the Jews were taken in captivity to Nebuchadnezzar's Babylon – "Babel" being the Hebrew name for the city. There they would have seen the "House which is the Foundation of Heaven and Earth", the mighty ziggurat built in honour of the god Marduk, a sight that must have deeply impressed them. Nevertheless, idolatry on such a scale would have appalled the unwilling immigrants, who felt nothing but distaste for life in the world's greatest city. The story of Babel was the result, combining a useful moral with contempt for Babylonian paganism.

But there is a much earlier reference to the curse of language. In the story of Enmerkar and the Lord of Aratta (see pages 64–65), Enmerkar's envoy tells of a golden age when "there were no snakes, there were no scorpions ... humankind had no opponents". In those days all the people could talk to their god Enlil in a single tongue. But Enki, god of magic and civilization, was unimpressed by the doings of humankind and chose to "estrange the tongues in their mouths".

Pieter Breughel the Elder's dramatic vision, painted in 1563, demonstrates the durability of the Babel legend through four millennia.

Lugalbanda's Ordeal in the Mountains

Not all of the tales about the feud between Enmerkar of Uruk and the Lord of Aratta involved magic and cunning. In one account, they waged war more conventionally with the spears and arrows of Uruk's elite troops. During the hostilities Lugalbanda, second of the Uruk's three great heroes, had a bizarre adventure on the road to the city of Aratta.

Sumerian literary tradition states that Lugalbanda, in his own right, was a god-king of the city of Uruk. He was generally held to be Gilgamesh's father, and according to the King List ruled the city for no fewer than 1200 years. But at the time of this particular adventure he seems to have been a young officer in Enmerkar's army commanding a division of Uruk's troops.

Halfway along the mountain road to Aratta, he was stricken with a strange, overpowering fever that baffled his companions. The best they could do as his teeth chattered in the cold was to find him a dry cave to shelter in.

There he lay deeply unconscious for so long that his companions feared that he might pass away while they went in search of help. So they prepared the crude cave as if for a funeral, laying out food and drink in the traditional Sumerian manner and placing his weapons beside him. If he lived, so much the better: he would have sustenance to give him strength. If he died, he would do so with dignity among the funerary goods and his companions would retrieve his body on their return from the campaign. With tears and lamentation, they left him to his fate.

But Lugalbanda did not die. After days laying unconscious in a coma he awoke. He was still feverish, and his barren surroundings appalled him. Brought up in the rich cities of Mesopotamia, the hostile mountains seemed to him a place of horror, so he prayed to the sun god Utu and his twin sister Inana: "In the mountain cave,

An inlaid panel (*c.*2650BC) shows Sumerian priests officiating at the sacrifice of a ram to the gods. Lugalbanda's companions left him with sacrificial food and drink which saved his life.

the most dreadful spot on Earth, let me be ill no longer! ... May my limbs not perish in the mountains."

The epic poet then goes on to make much of Lugalbanda's time of extreme distress: "A lost dog is bad, a lost man is terrible ... Let me not be thrown away into the desert! ... Let me not come to an end in the mountains like a runt!"

But Lugalbanda need not have feared for his life. Utu and Inana heard his pleas, and as a sign sent him a complex dream in which Lugalbanda found himself wandering through the mountains by moonlight. During this dream the god Zangara came to him in the form of a bull and hinted that he should capture the wild goats and, more importantly, the great bull of the mountains and offer them in sacrifice. "Who will melt their fat for me?" asked the god. "He should take my axe of tin, and my dagger which is of iron."

When Lugalbanda awoke, his fever had gone but the dream remained with him. As instructed, he took up an axe and dagger: "Like an athlete he brought away ... the wild bull of the mountains," and he offered it before the rising sun, along with the heads of the goats, "heaped up like barley-corns". The venomous snakes of the mountains smelt fresh blood in the air.

Lugalbanda's sacrifice symbolized the triumph of the city and its gods over the untamed creatures of the wilderness, as much as it demonstrated the warrior's piety. And the presence of the gods made the sacrifice "the shining place of pure strength". It was enough to restore Lugalbanda once again to health.

Here the ancient tablets crumble into silence and the remainder of the story breaks off. The remainder of it – how Lugalbanda finished his journey and perhaps how he returned in triumph to Uruk – is lost from this version, although a retelling of the myth suggests that he received an invaluable gift from the terrifying Anzu bird whom he had flattered in order to gain approval. That Lugalbanda was saved from the brink of death by the gods marks him as one of those "who have a place in Inana's heart ... who stand in the battle".

A wild goat rears up against a stylized sapling which may symbolize the Tree of Life in this Sumerian statue of about 2500BC. Lugalbanda was instructed by the gods in a dream to capture and sacrifice such an animal.

A Precious Gift from the Anzu Bird

Lugalbanda's adventures in the mountains gave rise to many dramatic stories. One of them tells how the hero, lost amid the high places, took the daring step of seeking out the nest of the fearsome Anzu bird, built near the eagle-tree of Enlil that grows from the summit of a vast mountain.

The Anzu was no ordinary bird. Vast and lion-headed, he presented a terrifying figure "At his cry the ground quakes ... in fear of him, wild bulls run away into the foothills, stags run away to the mountain". He was clearly not to be trifled with. So when Lugalbanda found the nest unguarded, with only a chick inside, he was careful to treat the young creature with respect. He fed it cakes and honey, salt meat and sheep fat, festooned its head with sprigs of white cedar and painted its eyes with kohl. He also decorated the nest, then cautiously retreated into a nearby hiding place in the mountains and waited.

Soon, as Lugalbanda had anticipated, the Anzu returned with his spouse, carrying a bull in his talons and another over his shoulder. He called out to his fledgling, but there was no reply. Fearing the worst, he and his mate uttered a cry of woe so piercing that it made the mountain gods "crawl into crevices like ants". But when the Anzu reached his nest, he found his child sitting quietly amid Lugalbanda's decorations. The parent bird was delighted: "Whoever has done this to my nest, if you are a god, I will befriend you. If you are a man, I will fix your fate."

At that, Lugalbanda came hesitantly forward and made a flattering speech to the Anzu. The bird was clearly pleased with this warrior who had befriended his offspring and offered to grant whatever wish was requested of him. So Lugalbanda asked for the ability to run anywhere he wanted without feeling fatigued; and the Anzu was as good as his word.

Lugalbanda's new skill meant that he could hurry back across the mountains to the siege of the city of Aratta and rejoin his comrades and his master Enmerkar who had given him up for dead. The conflict proved long and wearisome. A year passed but there was no sign of the defenders yielding. From the walls of Aratta "it rained down javelins as if from the clouds".

For Enmerkar, there was only one explanation: he had lost the favour of Inana. So he asked for a volunteer to carry a message back across the mountains to the goddess in Uruk. If she would allow him and his host to return in safety, he promised to put aside his spear and allow Inana herself to shatter his shield.

Lugalbanda, with his tireless legs, at once claimed the honour for himself. He decided to travel alone, despite the warnings of his comrades, who declared: "You will not come back from the great mountains, no one returns to humankind from there!" In fact, thanks to the power granted him by the Anzu bird, Lugalbanda reached Uruk before midnight on the same day, just as offerings were being made to the goddess in her temple.

He delivered his message, and Inana gave him her reply. She was not interested in Enmerkar giving up war. Instead, she told Lugalbanda, the king must cut down a solitary tamarisk tree that grew by one of the goddess's sacred pools. Then he should catch with his own hands a certain fish that lived there and offer it as a sacrifice. If this were done, victory over Aratta was assured and Enmerkar could return to Uruk with the spoils – the precious metal and stones for which he had gone to war in the first place.

The terrifying Anzu bird returns to its giant nest to find that its baby has been given a decorative crown of white cedar and had its eyes painted with kohl.

The Quest of a Superhero

Gilgamesh is the mightiest of the Mesopotamian heroes. Possibly based on a real-life king, he is portrayed in sculptures and reliefs from every period of the region's civilization as a robust, bearded warrior, who struggles with lions, bulls and assorted monsters. He owes his immortality to the great epic poem that came to be written about him – the very first such epic known to humankind.

Gilgamesh was probably an historical king of the Sumerian city of Unug (the Akkadian Uruk) early on in the history of Mesopotamia. It was said that he built the city with his own hands. However, some centuries later, he was being worshipped as a god at a number of Sumerian sites.

The extant tales about Gilgamesh start to appear around 2100BC, although the copies that have survived are mostly of a later date. The earliest stories, written in Sumerian, are all distinct episodes that the court poets of Ur probably would have based on versions that had circulated orally for centuries before their time. They are not very different from those legends describing the exploits of Lugalbanda and Enmerkar – far-fetched adventures with a great deal of action and frequent signs of godly favouritism.

The Epic of Gilgamesh itself, however, rises far above these origins. The crowning literary achievement of the Old Babylonian period and a work comparable to the *Iliad*, it was written in Akkadian around 1600BC. The principal version of the epic that has survived to this day, was recorded on twelve clay tablets by the Babylonian scribe and scholar Sin-lege-unninni around the year 1100BC. How much Sin-lege-unninni invented, and how much he collated from older material, we shall never know.

Further episodes have been assembled from a variety of archaeological sources, most of them

The imposing figure of the hero Gilgamesh is depicted gripping a lion cub on an Assyrian stone relief from the Palace of Sargon at Khorsabad in modern-day Iraq (*c.*800BC).

The Gilgamesh of History

Gilgamesh was no literary invention. The hero of the epic was based on a real king who ruled Uruk in about 2600BC, and whose prowess was the subject of tales circulating centuries before the poem was written. The Sumerian King List records him as the fifth ruler in Uruk's First Dynasty and provides him with the customary divine antecedents: his mother, it is said, was the goddess Ninsun.

Such divine ancestry was obligatory, for kingship in ancient Sumer was a blend of secular politics and religion. As ruler, Gilgamesh was *en* of the city. The word meant "lord", but had priestly associations too. The *en* was the conduit through which the city's gods spoke to their people. It was an intimate relationship: each year, the *en* went through a ritual marriage with the goddess Inana, who made Uruk her special charge.

The ceremony was also a way of ensuring the fertility of both the city's fields and its female inhabitants. A successful *en,* one who presided over abundant harvests and a contented population, could expect not only the citizens' loyalty while he lived, but even greater esteem after he died, when he would become a godlike figure to whom prayers and sacrifices might be offered.

Gilgamesh's role was not solely religious. He was also the military leader of a city state that was one among many jostling for supremacy. The political situation resembled that of classical Greece: no one city was strong enough to impose its will on all the others, but many were keen to try. To have thrived in such circumstances, Gilgamesh must have been skilled in battle and diplomacy.

Surviving historical records are non-existent, but the veneration accorded to Gilgamesh in Sumerian tradition suggests that he was successful in both roles. Long before the epic was written, religious writings testify to his deification, and he regularly features in tales of Uruk's military might. The kings of Ur's Third Dynasty, about 2100BC, liked to boast of their supposed descent from Gilgamesh, and by about 1800BC he was credited with having built the city's walls – which in fact predate his lifetime by at least one thousand years.

Gilgamesh demonstrates his legendary strength by raising a lion above his head, on this impression of an Assyrian cylinder seal from c.1350–1000BC.

fragmentary. Some are "official" copies of the epic from city archives, especially the great library of Ashurbanipal at Nineveh. Others may be the remains of assignments at Mesopotamia's many scribal schools: some tablets are clearly the work of student copyists, and there are variant readings. But we have reason to be grateful to these sometimes clumsy trainee scribes. The enormous quantity of cuneiform writing left behind means that although many tablets are badly damaged, they are seldom damaged in the same way, so it has been possible to reconstitute most of the text. There are irritating gaps here and there, and the surviving sections of the story do not connect in the way that their original authors perhaps intended. But the tale can be read in much the same form as the old Mesopotamians had it, and for the same reasons: for philosophical instruction in the ways of men and gods, of course, but also for sheer entertainment.

Heroes in Partnership

Far from being a mere relic, the *Epic of Gilgamesh* is one of the most dramatic stories ever told. Even today, 3500 years after its composition, its themes of friendship, loss and the fear of death have profound resonance. In Sumerian times, the epic must have enthralled its readers or, more often, its listeners – for in a society with only a tiny literate elite this poem was surely written to be read aloud.

The work begins with a bill of fare to whet the appetite of an eager audience. We are about to hear the adventures of someone special "who brought back a tale of times before the flood".

As Gilgamesh the hero quests for eternal life, he encounters episodes of sex and violence, love and death, friendship and parting. Naturally, like all great quests, this one ends in seeming failure. But in failing, the hero finds self-knowledge and comes of age.

This is a story – as the narrator is at pains to establish – rooted in the historical experience of the people of Mesopotamia. Indeed, the opening verses stress the immediacy of what is to follow: "Go up on to the wall of Uruk and walk around! Inspect the foundations, study the brickwork. Testify that its bricks are baked bricks."

Gilgamesh first appears as an historical ruler of the city of Uruk in Sumerian legend. He is recorded in the King List as the fifth king of the First Dynasty, son of the semi-divine Lugalbanda and the goddess Ninsun, making him "two thirds divine, and one third mortal".

Most of the poem's first section is a hymn to the virtues of the god-prince, superlative in his strength and as a warrior of great stature. In his city, "Uruk the sheepfold", he walked tall, a full five metres in height, according to a Hittite version of the epic. But for all his perfection, Gilgamesh had one debilitating flaw: a weakness for women. Although he was expected to be the shepherd of the city, he spent more time as a "rampant wild bull".

The goddess Ninsun, mother of Gilgamesh and wife of Lugalbanda, is shown sitting in a serene state on this Sumerian stone relief of the 3rd millennium BC.

The shaggy features of the wild man Enkidu (left) peer out from among his friends – the wild animals – on this Mesopotamian stone vase dating from *c.*3000BC.

The tablet states the problem bluntly: "Gilgamesh would not leave alone young girls, the daughters of warriors, the brides of young men."

Not surprisingly, the heavens rang with the complaints of the harassed women. Their noisy grievances did not go unheard. "Create a rival for him," the people prayed fervently to the mother goddess Araru, "someone to absorb his energies, and let Uruk be allowed peace!" The goddess listened and agreed to help.

So she took a lump of clay and made a double for Uruk's wayward ruler. She shaped Enkidu, a shaggy giant of a man, in the hope that he would combat Gilgamesh. In every way he was the opposite of the urban, sophisticated hero: "He knew neither people nor country; he was dressed as cattle are." Enkidu lived among the animals and knew their ways: he was, in fact, more animal than human, bonding with the creatures of the wilderness and sometimes saving them from the harsh snares of Uruk's hunters.

One such hunter, distressed by the sabotage of his animal traps and pits – and even more alarmed by the sight of Enkidu himself – went before Gilgamesh to seek assistance. "I am too frightened to approach him," he explained. "But he will not allow me to do my work."

Gilgamesh decided to use a subtle weapon against Enkidu: from his own experience, he knew of one likely weakness in the strongest of men. "Go," he told the hunter, "and lead forth the harlot Shamhat. She must take off her clothes and reveal her attractions." Gilgamesh predicted that once Enkidu had fallen for the prostitute's charms, he would lose his powers over the animals and they would become alien to him.

So it came to pass: the hunter took Shamhat out into the countryside, where the two lay in wait by a watering hole. After three days, Enkidu appeared as they anticipated. Shamhat, looking seductive with her breasts bared and undergarments carefully loosened, stepped boldly from her hiding place and everything happened as Gilgamesh foretold. "She did for him, the primitive man, as women do." For six days and seven nights, their lovemaking shook the Earth.

Afterwards, Enkidu discovered the price he had to pay for his passionate affair: the wild beasts who had been his friends fled from him, and when he tried to run after them he found his limbs had lost their former strength.

For Enkidu, this was a near-catastrophic loss of innocence. But there were compensations. Not only had he learned the pleasures of adult life, but he had acquired the rudiments of judgement – he had grown up. And if Shamhat had destroyed his youthful naivety, at least she offered him some compensatory enticements. First she flattered his manhood, and then she told him of the joys of city life. She explained that in Uruk the girls would show off their bodies to him, and a life of happiness awaited. Besides, in Uruk he would find Gilgamesh, "perfect in strength, like a wild bull", with whom he could find real friendship. Enkidu, seduced once more, agreed to go with Shamhat to the city. But

The Birth of Epic Poetry

When in the eleventh century BC the scribe Sin-lege-unnunni, working in the libraries of Nineveh, wrote down on twelve clay tablets the Gilgamesh cycle in its final, polished form, he created the world's very first recorded epic – and the conventions that he observed have been followed by his successors and continue to be so to this day.

The distinctive stamp of the epic genre is the way in which the hero almost always occupies the centre of the story, and Gilgamesh conforms with this. The poem is not ultimately about the fate of cities, kingdoms or civilizations, but about the destiny of just one man. The narrative may digress on occasions – to describe the creation of Enkidu, for example, or the Great Flood – but it always returns to the actions of its hero, as he matures from a relatively uncomplicated "death or glory" warrior to the pensive seeker after immortality we see in the epic's later sections.

Dreams play a major part in the plot, as is to be expected from a society that saw them as messages from the gods. The dream material is, often presented in a terse style that cranks up the dramatic tension of the story. By contrast, the speeches of gods and men alike are given at some length, in a declamatory style marked by frequent repetition. Ultimately, the writers are conscious of their duty to tell a good story: whatever the moral message they are trying to get across, however grand their theme, their role is to entertain.

In later times, Greek, Indian, Arab and European poets were to adopt surprisingly similar techniques in works as various as the *Odyssey*, the *Bhagavad Gita*, the *Aeneid* and *Beowulf*.

The Babylonian account of the Flood was recorded on the 11th tablet of the Epic of Gilgamesh. The story dates back to the 7th century BC and was probably the source of the biblical version in Genesis.

Thought to represent the hero Gilgamesh, this Assyrian terracotta statue of the 7th century BC was probably buried in the foundations of a house to protect it against evil spirits.

he added that, if Gilgamesh really was like a wild bull, he would have to challenge him.

So Shamhat dressed Enkidu in some of her own clothes and led him towards Uruk, where Gilgamesh was already having baffling premonitions that presaged the wild man's arrival. In the first dream, a thunderbolt fell to the ground and Gilgamesh could not lift it. In the second, a copper axe was thrown into an Uruk street, and the dream-figure of Gilgamesh presented it as an offering to his mother, the goddess Ninsun. She interpreted the visions for Gilgamesh: thunderbolt and axe alike represented a man, great in strength, whom Gilgamesh would learn to love.

Meanwhile, en route for Uruk, Enkidu and his harlot stopped for a few days at a shepherds' camp, where the delighted giant discovered bread and beer: another stage in the civilizing process was completed. This indulgent interlude in the story comes to an end when a young man rushes past. "What's the hurry?" asks Enkidu. "A wedding is about to take place in the city," the young man explained, "and Gilgamesh is expected to exercise his *droit de seigneur* over the bride."

Incensed by this information, Enkidu set off directly for Uruk and the wedding-house. When he reached the city, he caused a sensation among the local people. "He is just like Gilgamesh," they cried. "Mountains gave birth to him!" They rejoiced that the gods had found a perfect match for their ruler. When Gilgamesh approached the house, Enkidu barred his entry, and the two engaged in a furious battle before an awestruck crowd of citizens: "As wrestlers they grappled and crouched. They demolished the doorframe. The wall shook."

To Gilgamesh's dismay, he could not prevail over a man built so strongly that he resembled the battlements of the city, and Enkidu won the contest. But in his victory, the wild man yielded magnanimously to the loser. "Your mother bore you to be unique," Enkidu told Gilgamesh. "Enlil decreed that you should be king." And he raised Gilgamesh from the dusty ground, and they kissed each other and became friends.

A Companion for Gilgamesh

For the inhabitants of Uruk, this reconciliation was a huge relief. Gilgamesh was much less interested in the women of the city. It was just as his dream prophesied: at last he had found a mighty partner, a man whose companionship he would come to cherish almost as much as marriage.

After a while, however, Enkidu began to pine. The comforts of city living, prostitutes included, did not seem to agree with him. He was reduced to tears of rage and frustration, and, even worse, his strength began to fade away.

But Gilgamesh knew the answer to his friend's problem: they needed an adventure, and he had one in mind. Far away to the west, deep in the mighty forests, lived a monstrous being called Huwawa. Gilgamesh proposed to Enkidu that they should search for him and end his life.

Hunting the Forest Monster

Gilgamesh's proposed adventure did not immediately appeal to Enkidu. Unlike his friend, to whom Huwawa was simply a name, Enkidu had actually seen the monster, back in the days when he had run wild in the woods. He knew what they were letting themselves in for. "His utterance is fire. His breath is death. Why do you want to do this?" he asked. Besides, it was the great god Enlil who had appointed Huwawa as guardian of the forest. "It is an impossible challenge," Enkidu declared.

Gilgamesh was determined to pursue the monster, despite his companion's doubt. In heroic style he declared: "If I should fall, I shall have won fame. People will say, 'Gilgamesh grappled with ferocious Huwawa. He was nobly born.'" He then reproached Enkidu for his lack of fighting spirit.

At the same time he had an incentive to offer: the smiths of Uruk would forge for the friends mighty weapons, the greatest swords and axes ever seen. Stung by Gilgamesh's jibes and impressed by the promise of fine new weaponry, Enkidu agreed to take part in the expedition westwards. Before they left, the two were feted by the councillors of Uruk, who offered some sterling advice: "Do not rely, Gilgamesh, on your own strength. Keep your eyes sharp and guard yourself! Let Enkidu walk ahead of you ... " Enkidu was renowned for his familiarity with the forest paths and the tricks of Huwawa. It was he who would be able to guide Gilgamesh in the hostile forest.

The journey to the west was arduous and long – "the new moon to the full moon, then three days more" – and during the course of the expedition Gilgamesh was troubled by several ominous dreams. In one, he saw the adventurers fallen "like flies" at the foot of a mountain; in another, Heaven cried out and the Earth groaned. But Enkidu found a favourable interpretation. He explained the meaning of the dream to his friend: Huwawa, he prophesied, would lie dead at their feet.

They continued to Huwawa's forest, where the monster greeted them scornfully: "The fool Gilgamesh and the brutish man ought to ask them-

This grisly terracotta image of Huwawa dates from around 2000BC. The forest monster was feared even by Enkidu, who was familiar with the ways of the wilderness.

The Humiliation of Akka

One of the oldest legends about Gilgamesh – long predating the epic that bears his name – tells how he defeated the neighbouring city of Kish. The story is probably based on one of the many historical wars between the city-states of Sumer.

War began when Akka, King of Kish, sent envoys to Uruk demanding submission. Gilgamesh called the city elders together to discuss their response. He, of course, favoured resistance, but the elders, nervous of Kish's power, advocated surrender. An assembly of the city's fighting men agreed with Gilgamesh, however, and ordered Uruk's defences to be made ready.

Soon afterwards, Akka arrived at Uruk and besieged the city with an army large enough to dismay the defenders. But Gilgamesh was not intimidated. He told Enkidu, who again appears in this tale as his right hand man, to gather weapons for a show of strength that would so startle Akka "that his wits would become confused".

Gilgamesh also sent his bodyguard Birhurture to the camp of the enemy king. As soon as he stepped outside Uruk's gates, Birhurture was seized by the Kish soldiery and brought before Akka. At that point, the cupbearer of Gilgamesh peered out over the battlements of Uruk. "Is that man your king?" Akka asked Birhurture. Scornfully, the bodyguard replied, "Were that man my king, would not all foreign troops be overwhelmed, would not the mouths of the land be filled with dust, and would not Akka be captured in the midst of his troops?"

For his insolence, Birhurture received a beating. But now Gilgamesh himself "in terrifying splendour" mounted the walls of Uruk. The gates were thrown open and the city's soldiers, led by Enkidu, emerged in full battle order. Alarmed, Akka pointed to the battlements and cried to Enkidu: "Is that man your king?" Enkidu replied, "That man is indeed my king." And so, after a brisk fight, Akka the king of Kish was taken captive, fulfilling Birhurture's prediction. Generously, Gilgamesh spared Akka's life and confirmed him in his titles.

For many years, the kings of Babylonia took the title "King of Kish" after the legendary days of Kish's independence.

Gilgamesh musters an army of warriors to defend their mighty city of Uruk and to do battle against King Akka of Kish.

Gilgamesh and Enkidu kill the Bull of Heaven and other monsters on this impression from a Mesopotamian cylinder seal of *c.*2300BC.

selves why they have come to see me." He intended to bite through their necks, he declared, and leave their bodies to the birds of prey.

Gilgamesh's nerve almost failed him, but once more he was encouraged by Enkidu: "Don't turn back! Make your blows fall harder!" The combat was fast and furious, accompanied by terrible storms, while the land itself was split apart by their wrestling. In the end, Huwawa lay prostrate at Gilgamesh's feet, pleading for mercy.

The Monster Meets a Violent End

Gilgamesh was inclined to grant a reprieve for Huwawa. But Enkidu, his early reservations forgotten, disagreed with his companion: "My friend, catch a bird and where do its fledglings go?" he said cryptically. "Finish him off, slay him, grind him up." So Gilgamesh stabbed Huwawa and Enkidu struck off his head.

It was a deed they would both have cause to regret – they had forgotten that Huwawa was the appointed forester of Enlil; the god was bound to avenge his servant. But for the moment, all was triumph. Gilgamesh and Enkidu returned to Uruk elated by their glorious conquest.

Back in his own city, Gilgamesh washed his filthy hair and cleaned his gear. He put on his best clothes and his crown, cutting quite a dash for the women of Uruk. Mortal females were not the only ones to fall under his spell. The goddess Ishtar herself, protector of Uruk, was also greatly impressed, and she was nothing if not direct: "Come to me, Gilgamesh, and be my lover! Bestow on me the gift of your fruit." The goddess went on to recite a long list of advantages that she would bring as a wife – a chariot of gold and lapis lazuli for a start. And best of all, "Kings, nobles, princes will bow down beneath you!"

Clearly, Gilgamesh was on difficult ground. He had already offended Enlil; so he had to handle Ishtar with some tact. But fresh from his triumph over the Huwawa, the young prince was in no mood for diplomacy, not even with a goddess. He haughtily rejected her proffered favours.

What is Ishtar, he asked himself? "A draughty door that can't keep out winds and gusts. A palace that rejects its own warriors." He went on to compare her to a leaky waterskin, a battering-ram that destroys its own city wall, and an ill-fitting shoe. Worse still, he referred to the goddess' chequered past. "Come", he said cruelly, "let me describe your lovers to you." One by one, he enumerated the evil fates that had befallen those who succumbed to Ishtar's charms.

Such a litany would have outraged the most patient of women, and Ishtar was predictably furious. She went at once to her father, the sky god Anu, crying out, "Father, Gilgamesh has spelled out my dishonour." Anu mildly pointed out that if she was so angry, she should have dealt with Gilgamesh herself. But Ishtar wanted something special by way of revenge: the Bull of Heaven. She threatened that if Anu would not let her have it, then she would raise up the dead, so that they could eat the living and outnumber them.

Anu warned his daughter that the Bull of Heaven would bring seven years of famine to Uruk. But when Ishtar claimed to have put aside a store of grain to overcome hardship, Anu had to grant her request.

At first, the Bull lived up to its reputation. When it snorted near the river of Uruk, a chasm opened, swallowing one hundred young men. It snorted again, and two hundred or three hundred young men fell into it. When its next snort created a third chasm, Enkidu himself fell into it.

But Enkidu understood cattle, however fierce. He leapt from the chasm and seized the bull by the horns, so that it could only blow spittle into his face. Enkidu shouted to Gilgamesh to plunge his sword between its horns and neck tendons. Enkidu distracted the bull by seizing its tail, Gilgamesh took a mighty swing at the great beast and it fell to the ground.

Ishtar was beside herself with rage: "That man Gilgamesh who reviled me has killed the Bull of Heaven." But Enkidu was not at all impressed. Ripping off a limb from the dead animal limbs, he threw it into Ishtar's face threatening to do the same to her. To add insult to injury, Gilgamesh called to the craftsmen of Uruk to admire the colossal horns of the beast, and to prepare them for gilding. They were to hang, he said, as a trophy above his bed.

The two heroes washed themselves in the Euphrates, then rode in triumph through the city. It was their finest moment. "Who is proudest among the men?" Gilgamesh asked his retainers. And then he celebrated in his palace.

But while his admirers were sleeping off their carousing, Enkidu had a dream, the most ominous so far. The gods were consulting together and, on awaking, he suspected he knew the reason why.

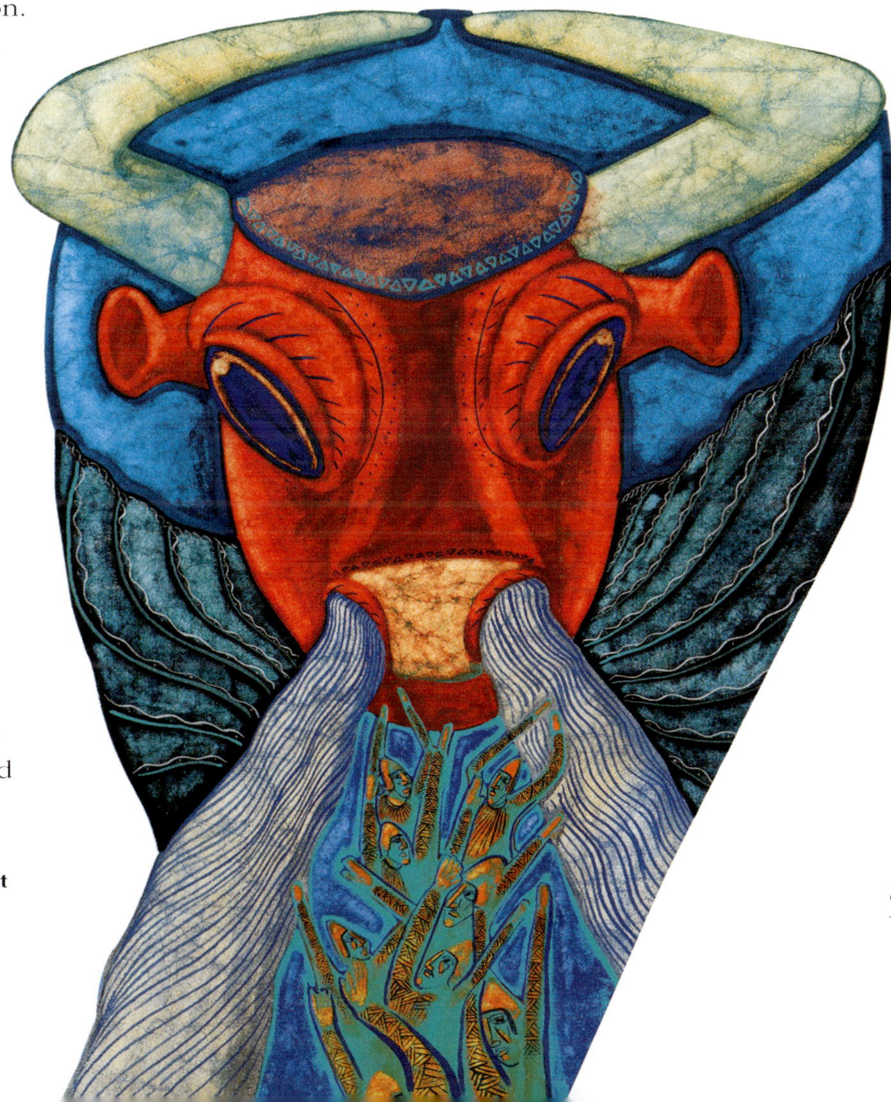

When the fearsome Bull of Heaven snorts, a chasm large enough to swallow one hundred men opens up. So to exact her revenge, Ishtar borrowed him from the gods.

Enkidu Pays the Price

The killing of Huwawa, the humiliation of Ishtar and the slaughter of the Bull of Heaven were insults that the gods were unlikely to pass over lightly. And so it was that Enkidu's dream turned out to be a true prophecy of coming events.

In the dream, the gods discussed the overweening pride of the two heroes and planned an appropriate punishment. The sky god Anu, smarting at the loss of his mighty bull, insisted that one of them die. "Let it be Enkidu," said Enlil, remembering his slaughtered steward. After awaking, Enkidu was distraught, not only at the prospect of his own death, but because he would have to part from Gilgamesh. "O my brother," Enkidu wailed, "they are taking me away from you." "They have left a legacy of grief for the next year," Gilgamesh replied. He prayed to Heaven for help, but in vain.

There was to be no heroic deathblow for his friend: Enkidu's end crept nearer in the form of a debilitating sickness while he railed against his fate. Remembering the happy innocence of his wild days in the woods, he cursed the hunter who first saw him, the harlot Shamhat who seduced him and the walls of Uruk themselves.

Then the sun god Shamash intervened. Enkidu had no right to curse the harlot:

"Who fed you on food fit for gods,
Gave you ale to drink, fit for kings,
Clothed you with a great robe,
Then provided you with Gilgamesh?"

Enkidu was ashamed: these were indeed great gifts. As he weakened, he retracted his curse on Shamhat and replaced it with a blessing.

But for Enkidu, the outcome was inevitable. Slowly he wasted away, and on the twelfth night he died. The following dawn, Gilgamesh could not believe that his friend was gone. "Now what is this sleep that has taken hold of you? Turn to me, you! You aren't listening to me!" For six days and seven nights he wept over his friend, refusing even to permit the rites of burial until, horribly, "a worm fell out of his nose".

A great change now came over Gilgamesh. Once he had believed it was enough for a man to leave a good name behind him: had he not told Enkidu, on the eve of their journey to meet the Huwawa, "If I should fall, I shall have won fame?" Back then, he had also said, "Humankind can number its days. Whatever may be achieved, it is only wind." Now, faced with the terrible reality of a death, he began to understand that such heroic

This horned cap is thought to symbolize the sky god Anu and the omnipotent Enlil, who decreed Enkidu's end. It was found in Babylon and dates from *c.*1120BC.

The Sacred Marriage

According to the Mesopotamian worldview, the sole purpose of man's existence was to serve the gods. And the best way to do this and to ensure divine favour was through the scrupulously accurate performance of prescribed rituals.

One of the most important ceremonies of the time was the traditional sacred marriage between earthly kings and the goddess Inana. The three greatest heroes of Uruk – Enmerkar, Lugalbanda and Gilgamesh – were all described as "bridegrooms of Inana", and their union with the goddess played a decisive part in their stories. Indeed, when Gilgamesh was foolish enough to reject Inana's advances (pages 82–83), he precipitated both the death of his closest friend and his own obsessive quest for immortality.

Although the three heroes all claimed a privileged relationship with Inana, the status of divine bridegroom was something they shared with the king of every Sumerian city-state. Each New Year's Day, a ritual marriage between ruler and goddess confirmed the structure of temporal power and ensured the goddess's favour in the months to come. Naturally, it was also the occasion for great public celebration and feasting.

Surviving texts of these rituals have both charm and a steamy intimacy. Thus at one ritual wedding Inana welcomed her suitor in these forthright terms: "My parts are well-watered lowlands ... Who will put plough oxen to them?"

In fact, the ceremony may have involved actual sexual congress. For ritual purposes, the king temporarily assumed divine status, and the symbolic marriage was celebrated in poems in which the king took on the role of Inana's husband.

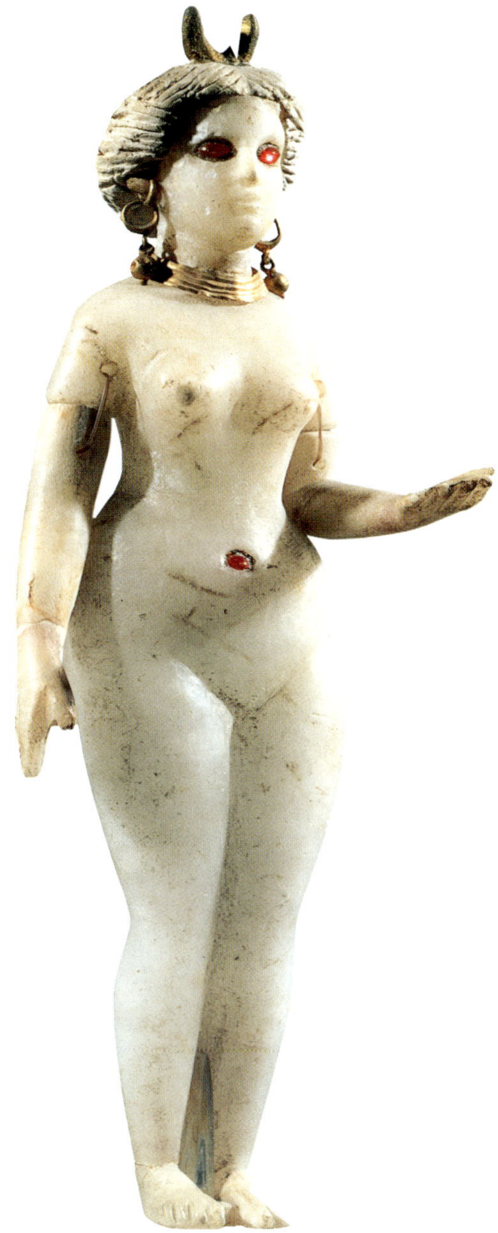

The seductive goddess of love was a favourite subject for Babylonian craftsmen. This statuette dates from the 3rd century BC.

attitudes are meaningless. It dawned on him that he too was mortal. He roamed the countryside around Uruk, sick with apprehension at the thought of his own extinction. "Shall I die too? Am I not like Enkidu? Grief has entered my innermost being. I am afraid of death."

The epic of Gilgamesh might have ended at this point. Instead, the story sets off in a new and rather different direction. Perhaps, Gilgamesh thought, a way may be found to defeat death. Searching his memory, he recalled the story of Ut-napishti, one of his own distant ancestors. This man had stood before the gods' assembly and sought eternal life. Might it be possible to discover immortality as he had done?

For Gilgamesh, it was no longer a matter of merely seeking adventure. No longer was he to battle with men and monsters for the sake of fame: now he waged war with death itself, and eternal life was the prize. A journey to find Ut-napishti had to be the first step.

The Journey towards Immortality

Gilgamesh's distant ancestor Ut-napishti was the only human being to ever become immortal. After Enkidu's death Gilgamesh determined to track him down and find out his secret. Ut-napishti lived at the end of the Earth, so Gilgamesh's journey was extremely hazardous. He set off, heading west across the mountains towards the mighty portal that opens each night to admit the sun.

The main portal to the Underworld was guarded by a frightful scorpion-man and his wife, "whose glances were death". Gilgamesh was rightly afraid, but nevertheless greeted them courteously. The scorpion-man, recognizing something unusual about the traveller, declared, "His body is flesh of the gods." His wife, echoing a phrase from the very beginning of the epic, described him as "two-thirds divine, one-third mortal". But when they both heard that Gilgamesh intended to go through the night tunnel of the sun they advised against it. The journey, through utter darkness, was quite impossible, they said.

Nonetheless, they allowed Gilgamesh to proceed. After long hours in impenetrable darkness, he burst into the bright sunlight of a magical valley that was delightful to his eyes. He walked through jewelled bushes and thorns down to the shore of a great sea. There he encountered Siduri the ale-wife, surrounded by her brewing vats and other objects of her trade.

A frieze of gods and animals provides symbolic protection to the grant of land described on this Babylonian boundary stone of 1100BC.

The sight of Gilgamesh – lean, weathered and wearing only a lion-skin – alarmed her; and at first, fearing that he might be an assassin, she locked him out. But she became more sympathetic when he told her about Enkidu's death, his overwhelming grief and the mission he had set himself.

He told her that since Enkidu's death he had set out in search of eternal life: "I keep wandering like a bandit in the open country. Now that I have found you, ale-wife, may I not find the death I dread." However, when Gilgamesh asked her to tell him the way to Ut-napishti's dwelling, she tried to dissuade him. Ut-napishti, she explained, lived across the sea, but the waters were lethal to the touch and there was no ferry; only the sun god could cross over. She also offered him some sound advice: "You will not find the eternal life that you seek. When the gods created humankind, they appointed death to the race."

But in face of Gilgamesh's urgent pleading, she relented. "There *is* a boatman," she told him, "a servant of Ut-napishti himself. This man, named Ur-shanabi, may be able to help. Go and let him see your face. If it is possible, cross with him. If it is impossible, retreat!" Gilgamesh would recognize the man, she explained, because of the curious "things of stone" he had with him.

Ur-shanabi was working in the forest when Gilgamesh located him. The encounter began awkwardly when Gilgamesh, mad with impatience, seized the boatman and broke the stone objects during the struggle. But then calm prevailed, and Ur-shanabi settled down to listen to his story.

Gilgamesh began immediately to tell of his fear "My friend whom I love has turned to clay. Am I not like him? Must I lie down too, never to rise, ever again?" Sympathizing with the hero's quest for immortality, Ur-shanabi told him how they might cross the treacherous sea in order to reach the safety of shore. The "things of stone" which Gilgamesh had damaged were punting poles used to pass over the water without touching it. So the hero had to cut 300 replacements from the forest – for since they were of wood, not stone, each one could be used only once and then had to be discarded. With careful punting, they would be able to traverse the most dangerous stretch of the waters.

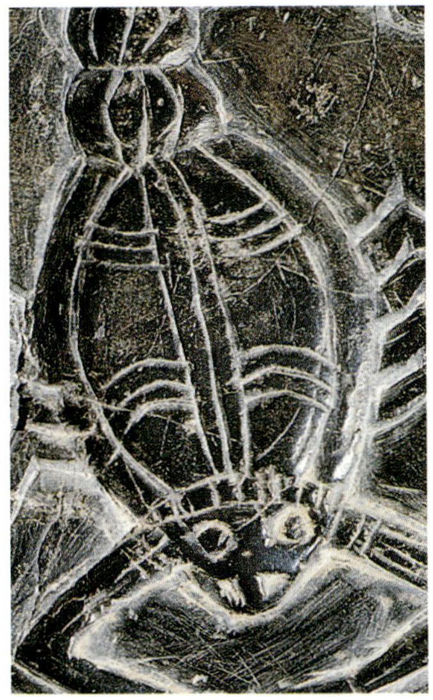

The scorpion, seen here on an 11th-century BC Babylonian carving, was a powerful protective symbol in Mesopotamia.

The plan succeeded but only just, as every single pole had to be used. Gilgamesh's mission appeared to be very close to completion. On the far shore, Ut-napishti was waiting for him, alive and well despite his immense age. He looked out in surprise and perplexity at the strange sight of a visitor. At last, the coveted secret of eternal life seemed to be within Gilgamesh's reach.

God-given Dreams

Dreams were taken seriously in Mesopotamia. They were almost always regarded as prefiguring the future, and sometimes even as a personal communication from a god. At best, they gave a warning that a wise man could act upon; at worst, they at least granted the dreamer time to reconcile himself to an impending and irrevocable doom.

In the Gilgamesh epic, as in many of Mesopotamia's heroic tales, dreams play a decisive role in the plot. Most of the key incidents of the epic – the successful fight with the monster Huwawa, for example, and the death of Enkidu, which sends Gilgamesh reeling off on his quest for immortality – are foreshadowed in dreams. In the the original text, these are often described at greater length than the actions that ensue.

The dream sequences also give a powerful impulse to the poem's narrative flow: how, the reader wants to know, will these cryptic prophecies be fulfilled?

Dreams were one of the few experiences that ordinary Mesopotamians could share with the great and the legendary. But even though almost anyone could take a dream-glimpse into the future, it was a specialist's job to elucidate their true meaning. The practice of interpreting dreams was the vocation of a specially trained class of priests, who were able to explain their significance to the unenlightened and offer suitable advice after the analysis.

Kings, of course, could go straight to the top. Thus when Gudea, ruler of Lagash in about 2140BC, was told in a dream to rebuild the ruined temple of his city, he checked his interpretation of the vision with the goddess Nanshe herself. Only when she gave her approval did he launch into a full-scale reconstruction programme. Little of Gudea's ancient temple now survives – except for the very inscriptions that explain to posterity just what made the king undertake the task.

Gilgamesh and the Flood

After a dreadful journey in which his wits had been tested and proven, Gilgamesh's hopes of gaining immortality were high. But they were almost immediately dashed. Pityingly, Ut-napishti told him that his long search has been in vain.

Ut-napishti's ark, which saved humankind from extinction, was unusual in size and shape and filled with every type of animal so that the world could be repopulated after the flood.

"Since the gods made you from divine flesh and the flesh of humankind, death is inevitable at some time, both for Gilgamesh and for a fool," Ut-napishti warned his visitor. But death was clearly not a threat to Ut-napishti, who, despite his great age, was still in perfect shape. "I look at you," Gilgamesh said to the sole human immortal, "and you are just like me." "Let me reveal to you a closely guarded matter," and Ut-napishti told Gilgamesh the story of the Flood. It is remarkably similar to the account of Noah in the Book of Genesis, so close that both versions must have sprung from the same original source.

Long before, when Ut-napishti lived in the ancient city of Shuruppag, the gods, after repeated efforts to reduce the human population, decided to finish it off for good by flooding the Earth. As already seen in the variant version of this myth described on pages 53–55, the god Enki was expressly forbidden to reveal the plan to the human race, but did so indirectly by addressing a reed hut. "Reed hut, brick wall, listen, reed hut, and pay attention, brick wall."

Just like Atra-hasis in the other version of the story, Ut-napishti was sitting on the other side of the wall. He listened carefully while Enki gave a list of detailed instructions. "Dismantle your house, and build a boat with harmonious dimensions. Leave your possessions behind, and fill the boat with the seed of all living things."

And so it was done. Ut-napishti's ark was vast in circumference, cube shaped with six decks. In due course the vessel, loaded with the seed of all living things as well as Ut-napishti's kin, was completed, and only just in time. For six days and seven nights, a tempest raged over the Earth. On the seventh day, Ut-napishti looked from his ark and saw that "all humankind had returned to clay. The flood plain was flat as a roof."

After a while the ark came to rest on the top of a mountain, and Ut-napishti released a dove. But the bird came back, for it had found nowhere to perch. Next, he released a swallow, with the same result. But on the third day, he sent off a raven, and the bird did not return: it seemed as though the floodwaters were receding.

"No one should have lived through the destruction!" shouted the furious Enlil. But Enki calmed him down. Sinners and criminals should certainly be punished, he conceded, but wiping out every living thing on the Earth was excessive.

Symbols of Untamed Power

The domestication of wild cattle was a huge advance for civilization. And in the days when the first cities and communities were developing on the fertile soils between the rivers, it was not so far in the past that people took it for granted. Although the beasts had been mastered, they were capable at any time of escaping all constraint. The bull, with its aggressive masculinity, was much celebrated in Mesopotamian art as a symbol of power.

In mythology the bull was usually linked closely with the storm god Ishkur (Adad); thunderclouds were often described as "bull calves". The Bull of Heaven that features in the Gilgamesh epic was one of the most dangerous weapons of the gods, not to be unleashed without good reason. At the same time, Anu himself, sky god and chief among the creators, was sometimes referred to as the "fecund breed-bull". And statues of a man-headed bull, sometimes equipped with wings, are found all over Mesopotamia, often serving as gatekeepers.

Right from the Early Dynastic period – that is, well before the historical Gilgamesh was ruling Uruk – the mysterious figure of a bull-man, human above the waist and taurine below, appears frequently in seals and clay reliefs. The creature was known as "kusarikku", according to some scholars the word also used for the Mesopotamian bison, which became extinct some time before the first flourishing of Sumerian culture.

Perhaps this association with a great beast now vanished from the Earth brought special powers; at any rate, the bull-man endured long into the Assyrian era, by which time he had evolved into a friendly demon whose protective powers could shield buildings and their occupants from evil.

This alabaster statue of a human-headed bull dates from the 3rd millennium BC and represents a magically protective demon.

Enlil allowed himself to be convinced, and the entire council of the gods eventually came to appreciate just how much was owed to Ut-napishti. Such bravery deserved a reward. So Enlil brought Ut-napishti and his wife before the assembled gods and blessed them with immortality.

Defeated by Sleep

But this extraordinary tale contained no shred of hope for Gilgamesh, as Ut-napishti was quick to point out. "Who can persuade the gods on your behalf?" he asked. Indeed, he planned to teach Gilgamesh a lesson. If the hero wanted to conquer death, then let him first try to conquer sleep, surely a much easier task. Ut-napishti challenged him to stay awake for six days and seven nights.

But Gilgamesh failed. Ut-napishti declared scornfully to his wife, "Look at the young man who wants eternal life! Sleep breathes over him like a fog." When Gilgamesh woke up, he was distressed: not only his struggle against sleep but his entire quest had ended in failure. "Wherever I set my foot, death is there too," he complained.

This was no more than Ut-napishti had told him already. But the immortal eventually took pity on Gilgamesh. The young man was in terrible physical condition, with filthy, matted hair. Ut-napishti ordered the boatman Ur-shanabi to wash him well, and for his return journey provide him with a set of magical clothes: they would stay clean "until he returns to his city".

A disconsolate Gilgamesh once more boarded the boat to recross the fatal sea. He was almost out of sight when Ut-napishti's wife chided her husband for his lack of generosity. "Gilgamesh came weary, striving. What will you give him to take back to his country?" Hearing this, Gilgamesh rapidly returned to the shore. Relenting, Ut-napishti told of a plant whose root resembled a camel-thorn. It grew deep underground in the *apsu* – the freshwater ocean under the Earth. "If you can win that plant, you will be rejuvenated."

Gilgamesh at once opened the gateway to the *apsu*, tied heavy stones around his feet and plunged in. He found the plant and returned to the surface in high spirits. At last he had something to make his long ordeal worthwhile. As he told the boatman, "This is a plant to cure a crisis!" With uncharacteristic caution, however, he decided to take it back to Uruk with him. "I shall give it to an elder to eat, and so try out the plant," he said.

But it was not to be. On the way home, he and Ur-shanabi stopped for the night by a pool of cool water. Gilgamesh, hot and weary, decided to

The Death of Gilgamesh

An alternative conclusion to the story of Gilgamesh has survived. This earlier, Sumerian account of the hero's end may enshrine the memory of a mass human sacrifice.

All that survives of the other death story are two fragments of a much longer poem. In the first fragment, Enlil warns the hero that he is not destined for immortality. In compensation, however, he has been granted supremacy over mankind during the rest of his lifetime, as well as invincible military skill. But die Gilgamesh must; and eventually, after many years of triumph, "He lies, he rises not."

In the next, apparently final section, Gilgamesh is already in the Underworld, amid the gods who live there and the shades of the illustrious dead who have

A 13th-century BC Assyrian relief depicts wooden boats perhaps similar to the one in which Gilgamesh travelled to the Underworld.

bathe. But while he was relaxing in the pool, a snake smelled the fragrance of the magical plant, came up silently and stole it away, simultaneously shedding its scaly skin. Seeing the useless pelt before him and realizing his loss, Gilgamesh broke down and wept. "For what purpose have my arms grown weary?" he asked the boatman. "I have gained nothing for myself, only for the serpent." And with that he gave up his quest. There was to be no eternal life for Gilgamesh, or any other man. Yet in his failure, he overcame the fear that had haunted him since the death of Enkidu, he became resigned to his own mortality.

Gilgamesh's journey ended where it had started, beneath the imposing walls of Uruk, where it is said he spent his last years beautifying the city. Even if he never achieved immortality, he was determined to live on in human memory.

preceded him. But he has not made his final journey alone, for we are given a long list of his companions, including his wives, his concubines, his musicians and entertainers, and even his valet. The text goes on to describe how Gilgamesh makes offerings to the gods of the Underworld to persuade them to accept the new arrivals.

Uruk, occupied for 5000 years, was surrounded by a 9.5-kilometre wall. It is said that Gilgamesh took great comfort in its construction.

In this list of names and rituals, we are probably reading an authentic description of a mass human sacrifice. The retinue that followed Gilgamesh on his final journey may well have been slaughtered to order.

Archaeology supports this grim interpretation. When Sir Leonard Woolley excavated the Royal Tombs of Ur, he found not only the bodies of Ur's rulers, but around them scores of retainers who had been killed so that they could serve their masters beyond the grave.

The Heroes Visit the Land of the Dead

Another story from the Gilgamesh cycle is not incorporated into the epic itself. It tells how Enkidu made a journey to the Underworld and returned with strange tales of the dead.

The gateway to the Sumerian Underworld was discovered in the most prosaic manner. Gilgamesh was playing an ancient Mesopotamian game that involved a playing stick, a *mekku*, and some sort of ball or puck, the *pukku*. We know little about this ancient sport, perhaps a precursor to hockey, but it seems to have been popular. *Pukku-mekku* was played at weddings, and may have been part of a fertility ritual – as well as being fun, of course.

In the tale, to the vexation of Gilgamesh, his *pukku* vanished down a hole. But he soon discovered that this was no ordinary hole: the lost *pukku* tumbled all the way to the Underworld. At once Enkidu, described in this tale as Gilgamesh's servant rather than his fellow adventurer, volunteered to go and recover it on behalf of his master. This was not something to be undertaken lightly, Gilgamesh warned him, for there were many prohibitions to be observed. To start with, "You must not put on a clean garment, for they will recognize you as a stranger." Enkidu was also forbidden to raise a club in his hand, to throw a stick or even to wear shoes, lest "the Earth's outcry seize you".

But Enkidu ignored his lord's instructions and for no apparent reason broke every single rule on the list. As a result, of course, "the Earth seized him" and he was unable to return to the surface. Despite Enkidu's disobedience, Gilgamesh went to great lengths to get him back. First he made offerings at the temple of Enlil, but was ignored. Next he went to the temple of Sin, but "Father Sin answered him not a word". At last, he went to the temple of Enki, where the god told him what to do: "Open up a hole in the Earth, so that the spirit of Enkidu can come out like a gust of wind".

During a game, Gilgamesh loses his *pukku* (puck) which plummets down into the previously undiscovered Underworld. Later, Enkidu went down to fetch it for him.

Gilgamesh duly opened the hole and, sure enough, the spirit of Enkidu came out of the Earth. The two embraced, overjoyed to see each other, and Gilgamesh asked to be told "the order of the netherworld which you saw". Here the tale takes a grimmer tone, for as Enkidu said, "If I tell you, you will sit down and weep. My body, which you touched and your heart rejoiced, is full of dust like a crevice." Enkidu nevertheless agreed to his master's request, and in response to a sequence of questions – "Did you see the man who had only one son?" "Did you see him who fell in battle" – he described the fate of the dead.

The news was not encouraging. The man with few offspring, for example, wept continually. As for the battle victim, he could not move; instead his father held his head in his lap and his wife mourned for him. A man with no known grave was destined to be eternally restless. Others fared better, especially those with children who could make suitable offerings on their behalf.

Very occasionally, the Underworld was a place of generosity. "Did you see my little stillborn children who never knew existence?'" "They play at a table of gold and silver, laden with butter."

But ultimately the Sumerian Underworld was depicted as a bleak, barren place, which perhaps explains the ferocious desire of Gilgamesh in the epic proper to shun death altogether.

A Dark and Dismal Place

For the Sumerians and their successors, the afterlife was usually a grim experience. The Underworld itself, thought to be situated even lower than the subterranean ocean of* apsu*, was a dark and dusty abode, which held few promises of pleasure after death.

The Sumerians had many names for the Underworld, but often called it simply "Earth", "ground', or even "the land of no return". Its ghostly inhabitants eked out an existence that was at best a pale replica of their previous Earthly lives.

According to the Sumerians, the dead spent most of their time wandering thirstily in the dark, with nothing better to eat than dust. Their Babylonian and Assyrian successors expected to be plagued by demons and monsters. The demons were thought to escape to the upper world, bringing suffering and sometimes death to mortals. Unusually, the denizens of the Mesopotamian Underworld also included dead gods, for immortality was hard to come by and gods could be slain.

But compared to other cultures, there was one ordeal the Mesopotamian dead were usually spared – a final judgement. Although the Underworld was presided over by the goddess Ereshkigal (with her consort Nergal), she seldom assessed the earthly conduct of the newly dead. Instead she ensured that their names were recorded by her chief scribe.

The bad probably went unpunished, and the just received little reward. Indeed, the Underworld seemed remarkably egalitarian. The shades of kings were not given superior status but shared the fate of commoners' shades. The only hope for life after death for people of any class was to have living relatives make offerings on their behalf.

On this neo-Babylonian bronze plaque the god Pazuzu (above) drives the evil demon Lamashtu (below) back to his rightful place in the Underworld.

KINGS AND PRINCES

The king's duties throughout the ancient Middle East included religious observances as well as affairs of state. Indeed, the Sumerians believed the king was chosen by the gods to be responsible for the people's welfare. For centuries the temple controlled the administrative business of the state, but gradually temporal power shifted to the palace. Although the kings were agents of the gods and had to perform various ceremonies, they were rarely, during the two and a half millennia of Mesopotamian hegemony, regarded as divine themselves.

Left: **Ginak was Prince of E-edin, presumed to be a border town in northern Mesopotamia. He wears a sheepskin skirt, a symbol of status that was reserved for ceremony.**

Above: **This sculpture of King Idrimi II of Alalah (*c.*1500BC) bears an inscription that tells how he fled to Aleppo, lived for a time in Canaan and came to be king of Alalah – a city north of Ugarit – as a vassal of the Hurrians.**

Left: **This granite portrait of King Gudea, ruler of Lagash, was carved *c.*2100BC. Lagash was a city state in the south of Mesopotamia that became independent after the collapse of the Akkadian empire.**

Above: Shalmaneser III (858–824BC), the Assyrian king, extended his empire as far west as Phoenicia, the home of these tribute bearers carved on a black obelisk.

Far left: This limestone statue shows Ashurnasirpal II (883–859BC) in a priestly role. The prefix Ashur- in several Assyrian kings' names refers to their chief god.

Left: A stele commemorating the victories of Naram-Sin (2254–2218BC). The ruler of an empire that stretched from the Mediterranean to east of the Gulf, Naram-Sin declared himself to be a god.

THE KINGDOM OF BAAL

The inhabitants of the city of Ugarit, on the coast of western Syria, belonged to a group of peoples known in the Bible as Canaanites. They were said to be closely related to the Phoenicians. The city was destroyed by invaders around 1200BC and remained lost to the world for over 3000 years. Then in 1928 a Syrian farmer ploughing a field near the modern village of Ras Shamra struck what turned out to be an ancient tomb. Archaeologists soon uncovered the ancient city. Since then, thousands of compositions transcribed on to clay tablets have been excavated in the area. These include legal and trading records, diplomatic correspondence with distant kings, medical recipes and multilingual dictionaries. This evidence suggests that Ugarit was a cosmopolitan city, a trading port that would have been visited by Mycenean, Egyptian, Hurrian, Hittite and Babylonian peoples.

Opposite: **A beautiful gold plate decorated with a hunting scene from cosmopolitan Ugarit (*c.*1400BC).**

The land known as Canaan covered large parts of modern Syria, Jordan, Lebanon and Israel, and the inhabitants of the various city-states had a similar language and culture. The country is the Bible's "promised land" destined for the Hebrews, and comparisons between the cultures and religions of the Jews and the Canaanites have revealed similarities. Even the literary style of the Ugaritic texts is close to that of the Old Testament.

Below: **This bronze statuette of the goddess Anat (who corresponds to Ishtar) was found in Ugarit (modern-day Ras Shamra) and dates from the 19th century BC.**

As scholars translated these texts it became clear that the character of the Hebrew god Yahweh shared much with earlier Ugaritic models. In the Judaic development of monotheism, Yahweh seems to have combined qualities of the older Canaanite deities El and Baal. However, in their eagerness to deny this connection and to emphasize the uniqueness of Yahweh, the Old Testament prophets denounced Baal as the false god of enemy tribes.

The Canaanite deities also have much in common with the Mesopotamian pantheon. El was the chief of the gods who upheld and enforced the institution of kingship. Elderly, wise and compassionate, he was usually portrayed as a remote figure, much like An, the reclusive father of the Mesopotamians. Baal was the god of the rainstorm and, like the Mesopotamian Enlil, was actively involved in battles and conflict.

Goddesses play a relatively minor role in the texts discovered so far, with the exception of Baal's sister Anat. She performed the crucial act of visiting the Underworld to rescue and resurrect her brother, which, together with her capricious and belligerent character, would suggest that she corresponds to the Mesopotamian goddess Inana who did the same for her lover Dumuzi.

The First Alphabet

On May 14 1929 at five o'clock in the afternoon, two French archaeologists made a dramatic discovery. Digging under a huge pile of volcanic ash and stones at the site of the ancient city of Ugarit, they uncovered the first of many baked clay tablets bearing compositions in a cuneiform script. This system of writing, created by pressing clay while it was still slightly wet with a reed stylus, was employed by various peoples from the end of the fourth millennium BC until about the first century BC. But what was so exciting about this particular find was that the script was completely unknown to the modern world.

Whereas cuneiform script from Mesopotamia consisted of many different symbols, representing a large range of syllables, the Ugaritic script contained only thirty signs. Scholars quickly realized that this was an early form of the alphabet, with each character representing a single letter. However, it still seemed impossible to decipher the texts since both the alphabet and the language itself were completely unknown to anyone.

The style of the painted pottery found in surrounding tombs suggested that the site could have been a Mycenean colony and the language a form of Greek. But scholars noticed that the words were separated from each other by a little vertical mark and that each word generally consisted of only three or four signs. This typical pattern of consonants was reminiscent of a Semitic language such as Hebrew or Arabic. This realization was the decisive breakthrough; the Ugaritic script was completely deciphered a year or two later. The earliest known alphabet, it already listed letters in the same order as modern-day equivalents and was presumably descended from still older models. One of the first Ugaritic words to be understood, because it stood at the head of so many columns of text, was Ba'al (the name of the god Baal).

The similarity between this Semitic language and Hebrew meant that once under way, the initial translation was speedy. Nevertheless, to this day, there are several important passages that remain extremely difficult to understand and to recount as a coherent story without having to refer to comparative languages. But the association with the Old Testament encouraged assumptions in determining meaning which eventually led to the distinctive worldview of the ancient Canaanite peoples being obscured.

The clay tablets containing the myths presented here were found in the library of the chief priest of Baal and were written around 1350BC by the scribe named Ilimilku. He signed them and added a postscript stating that he had copied them at the dictation of the chief priest Atanu-Purlianni. It seems reasonable to suppose that these tablets came from a representative collection of the most important religious texts. It also seems likely that they were used for recitation during rituals.

An Akkadian royal seal (*c.*1335–1310BC) inscribed with a treaty installing a certain Nigmepa as king of Ugarit.

Baal, a Stormy God

Baal ruled over storm clouds, rain, thunder and lightning. He was a restless being, constantly caught up in conflicts between the elements and the seasons. The myths about him tell of his struggle to defend his position as a king, and describe his death and resurrection – themes common to many divine figures in the ancient Near East.

The headdress and face of this 13th-century BC bronze statuette are overlaid with gold leaf. Silver on the chest and limbs may indicate armour. The figure is thought to represent Baal.

The Canaanite name Baal simply means "Lord" and there were several "Baals", worshipped in different localities. The Baal of Ugarit was also called Hadad and it seems that over time he had become the most dominant Baal in the region.

The series of myths about Baal are the most important surviving religious compositions from Ugarit. They are described on several clay tablets; many of these are damaged, which causes dispute among scholars who still question the order of events and the contents of the missing sections.

The myths constitute a chronicle of Baal's rise from a position of relative insecurity to one of pre-eminence among the gods. A key episode in the story concerns his demand to be allowed to build himself a palace – which represented both a king's dwelling place and a god's temple.

Baal was one of the sons of the chief god, the quiescent El. The younger god is portrayed in the cycle as growing in warrior prowess in his youth until he achieves kingship as an adult. But although he became increasingly important Baal never displaced El. While El presided in the pantheon, Baal's exploits were glorified as those of a younger and more vigorous god, always vulnerable to challenge and a reversal of fortune.

The story of Baal's rise may represent his role as patron god of the city of Ugarit, or it may reflect the increasing dominance of one of the many Canaanite tribal groupings, of which he was patron. The shift of power from an older sky god to a younger storm god is widely paralleled across the ancient world. For example, El was the god of Israel before he was displaced by Yahweh, while the Hittite god Kumarbi was superseded by his son Teshub (see pages 123–24) and the Greek Kronos was eventually usurped by his son Zeus.

Baal's growth in stature came about through his striving nature, which came to the fore in cosmic battles. Although there is mention of several monsters that he had previously defeated, the battles which are recounted in detail involved his brothers Yamm (the Sea) and Mot (Death), who were initially favoured above Baal by their father El.

A further aspect in the cycle concerns Baal's relationship with the goddess Anat. As his loyal and forceful sister, she supported his demand for a palace and rescued him from death. There also exist other, fragmentary texts which portray her in highly erotic language as his lover.

The Fight for Power

The central surviving Baal cycle revolves around two elements that were crucial in many mythologies: the struggle for power and the fertility of the Earth. The myth sets the two sons of El, Baal and Yamm, against each other. Initially, the powerful Yamm seems to have the upper hand.

The tablet which recounts the myth of Baal's struggles with his brothers is badly damaged and the sequence of events remains unclear. It seems that El, the father of the gods, had earlier favoured Yamm above his brother Baal by allowing Yamm to build himself an impressive palace, the distinguishing mark of a monarch. It seems that Baal then rose up in revolt against Yamm and sought backing from El and the other gods.

At the point where the text becomes legible, Yamm has just sent two messengers to El's court and given them the following instructions: "El, the chief of the gods, is protecting Baal. When you come before him and his council, do not prostrate yourselves but remain standing to deliver your message. Demand that he hand Baal over to me, so that I may inherit his gold!" So powerful and aggressive was Yamm that when the messengers arrived they found the gods already poised to capitulate, their heads sunk on to their knees in submission. The messengers remained standing to make their demand and they were very convincing. El told them to give Yamm this message: "Let Baal be your slave, Yamm. Like the other gods, he must submit to you."

But Baal was undaunted by their challenge. Seizing a weapon that was mounted on a nearby wall, he rushed forward to kill the messengers and was restrained only by the wise words of the two goddesses Anat and Athtarat, who reminded him that messengers were inviolable and it would be considered a serious crime to attack them.

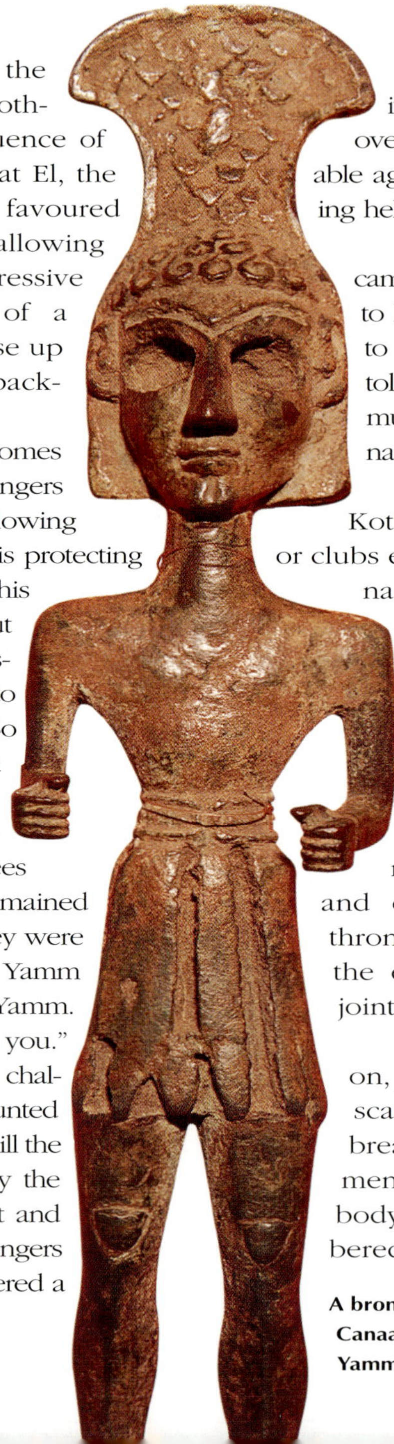

The tablet again becomes illegible but it seems that Baal was captured and handed over to Yamm. When the text becomes readable again Baal is in a wretched situation, cowering helplessly like a slave under Yamm's throne.

But the divine craftsman Kothar wa-Hasis came to Baal. He reminded him that his claim to kingship itself was at stake, and urged him to act. "Prince Baal, Rider of the Clouds," he told him, "you must smash your enemy, you must annihilate your foe. Take back your eternal royalty, your everlasting sovereignty!"

To give Baal the means to act, Kothar wa-Hasis fashioned a pair of maces or clubs endowed with magic powers. "I hereby name these the Chaser," he said. "Chase Yamm from his throne, fly from the hand of Baal like an eagle, drive him from the throne!" The Chaser danced from Baal's hand and struck Yamm on the shoulder. But Yamm withstood the brunt of the blow. Then Kothar wa-Hasis fashioned another mace, this time naming it the Expeller, and ordered it to oust Yamm from his throne. The Expeller struck Yamm between the eyes. This time Yamm staggered, his joints shook and he crashed to the ground.

The goddess Athtarat cheered Baal on, shouting, "Scatter him, mighty Baal, scatter him, Cloud Rider!" Here the text breaks off again, ending with a few fragmentary references to various parts of the body. These may mean that Baal dismembered Yamm, like the Babylonian Marduk

A bronze statuette of the supreme deity El, father of the Canaanite pantheon. He showed favouritism to his son Yamm by allowing him to build a palace.

Monsters of the Deep

Throughout the ancient Near East the sea was often portrayed as a formidable opponent manifest in the form of a dragon or serpent. Rivers similarly came to be seen as forces which, although useful to humanity, could become extremely destructive when untamed.

Baal was said to have defeated several sea monsters, including a serpent called Lotan, the Ugaritic spelling of the biblical Leviathan, while his sister Anat fought against a dragon who swirled and churned the sea with his twin tails as his double tongue licked the heavens.

In the Old Testament there are reports of a similar battle between Yahweh and the ocean in the form of a snake: "With his power he stilled the sea, and his hand pierced the fleeing serpent." (Job 26: 12–13) Baal's adversary Yamm, the Sea, was sometimes also called Nahar, the River – probably because, in the minds of Canaanites, the ocean and rivers were two aspects of one great body of water thought to encompass the universe.

This association of sea and river as a powerful threat to civilization appears in other, related traditions. At the beginning of the Babylonian *Enuma elish* (see pages 22–27) the two form a unity through the mingling of their waters. In the Old Testament, the parting of the Red Sea is echoed by the crossing of the river Jordan: "When Israel came out of Egypt, the sea saw and fled, the Jordan turned back." (Psalms 114: 1–3)

Baal struggles with a giant sea serpent called Lotan, whom he eventually defeated although the texts do not explain how.

in his battle with Tiamat (see pages 24–26). Alternatively, he may have taken Yamm's insignia and worn it on his own body, as Marduk did when he stripped the Tablet of Destinies from Qingu (see page 24).

A Residence Fit for a God

Following his victory over Yamm, Baal felt aggrieved that he still had no palace to call his own, like any other proper king. "Baal the rain god has no house like the other gods," he complained bitterly to his sister Anat, "no court like the other sons of his mother Athirat, to shelter his daughters Mist and Dew." Anat immediately went to their father El to intercede on her brother's behalf. Yet rather than approach him diplomatically, Anat threatened her father. If he did not give Baal a palace, she said: "I'll smash your head and smear your grey hair with blood!"

El was not at all perturbed by this outburst and calmly responded to his daughter's tyranny, "I know that you are hot-headed, my daughter. What is it you want?" Anat explained that Baal had become the most important god in the pantheon, yet was reduced to weeping because he did not have a palace of his own like the other gods.

El replied that he was unable to grant this privilege without the consent of his wife Athirat. In a ruse to ensure her agreement, he sent for Kothar wa-Hasis, ordering from him an array of exquisite furniture and ornaments made of gold and silver. When these had been made and delivered, Baal and Anat presented them to their mother, who was quickly won over. In giving her consent, Athirat made a remark that highlights the symbolic significance of Baal's palace, fit only for a king and provider of rain. "Now Baal will start the rainy season, the season of rivulets in flood," she declared, "He will thunder in the clouds, he will fling lightning bolts to Earth."

Baal was overjoyed and immediately sent out caravans of camels to bring back cedar from Lebanon and silver, gold and jewels from the mountains. He commissioned Kothar wa-Hasis to design and build him a palace extending for ten thousand hectares on the top of Mount Zaphon. No sooner was the palace finished than Baal proudly inaugurated it with a feast for the other gods. He then consolidated his position as king by setting out on a tour of the cities in his domain.

Baal Agrees to be Swallowed by Mot

After his disagreement with Kothar wa-Hasis

To help Baal, his sister Anat bribed her mother Athirat with beautiful objects made of gold. Some exquisite gold has been unearthed in the region such as this elaborate necklace (*c.*1750BC) found in a tomb at Ebla.

Death Enters through a Window

While discussing the architectural plans for the new palace, Baal and Kothar wa-Hasis disagreed about whether or not to include a window. Although Baal at first resisted the idea, he later changed his mind. His decision was to prove almost fatal, leading to a confrontation with Mot (Death).

Kothar wa-Hasis suggested a window in the royal palace and Baal opposed him. Baal was concerned that his daughters, Dew and Mist, would escape from the palace and fly away. Later Baal must have changed his mind and opted to have a window installed, which provoked words of reproach from Kothar wa-Hasis: "Did I not tell you, Baal, that you would come back to my words."

The final building did contain a window but its inclusion was to prove a terrible mistake. Although the opening allowed Baal to manifest his power over fertility by pouring rain on to the Earth, it also exposed him to Death, who, it was commonly believed, could only enter a house through a window.

When Baal returned from his triumphal tour of his kingdom he decided to open the window by making a gap in the clouds. Shouting through the opening, Baal managed to make the Earth below shake as he flung out a defiant challenge to Death: "Enemies of Baal, why do you tremble? Will any king or non-king establish himself on this Earth where I am sovereign? I alone reign among the gods, I alone feed the multitudes on Earth and make them fat!"

Baal followed up his challenge by sending two messengers, Gapan (Vine) and Ugar (Ploughed Field), down to Mot's realm in the Underworld. Baal gave his messengers careful instructions for their dangerous mission. "Go down into the dismal, desolate land where Mot reigns. But be careful as you approach him: don't give him a chance to seize you like lambs in his jaws. Go and tell him I have built my palace of gold and silver." The remainder of his message, like the account of the messengers' journey itself, is lost. But the boastful mention of Baal's splendid new palace with its window suggests that the tone was provocative and led to further confrontations between Baal and Death (see page 104).

Baal opens a window in his palace in the sky to release two messengers, Gapan and Ugar, with a provocative message for the god of Death.

(see page 103), Baal chose to send a provocative message to Mot who returned an equally menacing response: "My appetite is that of lions in the desert, or the longing of dolphins in the sea! So Baal, you have summoned me to eat food and drink wine! Ah, if only you would descend down my throat and into the abyss of my entrails!"

Here a large part of the text is missing, so that it is impossible to know how Baal shifted from an attitude of arrogance to one of submission in which he consented to be swallowed by Mot. But when the text resumes he has sent his messengers back to give Mot his greetings and relay this message: "Divine Mot! I am your eternal slave, I am yours for ever!'" Then Mot stretched his jaws until they were vast, and his tongue reached to the stars. Baal slipped down Mot's throat like an olive, taking with him all his rainmaking powers and his assistants: clouds, rain, thunder and lightning, as well as his daughters Mist and Dew.

Immediately the surface of the Earth fell into the grip of a scorching drought. The messengers Vine and Field reported to the other gods that they had seen Baal in the Underworld, lying dead on the ground. The compassionate El was overcome with grief. Coming down from his high throne, he sat on the ground and poured dust over his head. Ripping and tearing at his body, he "ploughed" his

Palace and Temple Ruins

A direct parallel between divine kingship and the status of kings on Earth is outlined in the myths. After all, Baal's earthly home was a temple, while on high he dwelt in a palace with his fellow gods.

The clay tablets containing the texts of the Baal cycle were found in the Temple of Baal, an earthly reflection of his celestial dwelling on the summit of mythical Mount Zaphon.

It has been claimed that the design of the Canaanite temples to Baal, such as that at Hazor, provided the model for the temple which Solomon later built in Jerusalem for Yahweh. Rejecting the Hebrews' traditional nomadic lifestyle, Solomon employed Phoenician architects and craftsmen to build both his home and his temple, which was consecrated with a prayer that could equally well have been uttered by a devotee of Baal: "Give rain to your land, which you gave to your people as their inheritance." (I Kings 8:36). This link with the hated Baal may explain the initial hostility of some prophets to the building of the temple: "Thus says Yahweh: 'Would you build me a house to live in? I have not lived in a house since the day I brought the Israelites out of Egypt, but I walked among them with a tent as my divine home ... Have I ever said to any of Israel's judges, "Why haven't you built me a house of cedar? "'"
(II Samuel 7:5–7)

These ruins represent the foundations of the once bustling Canaanite port of Ugarit. The main buildings in this city were the Royal Palace and a temple dedicated to Baal.

flesh by cutting furrows into it, and cried, "Baal is dead! What will become of his people?"

Baal's sister Anat was equally grief-stricken and her tears flowed into her mouth like wine. She too ploughed her flesh with her nails and then called upon the sun goddess Shapash to carry her the following night on her journey through the Underworld. With her bright rays Shapash located Baal's lifeless body and balanced it on Anat's shoulders. Together at sunrise they lifted him up to the summit of his own mountain of Zaphon, where they buried him and made animal sacrifices.

In the absence of Baal, the drought continued. His parents El and Athirat looked for a substitute among their other sons and tried to give Baal's throne to the ambitious Athtar. But Athtar was so inadequate that his feet would not even reach down to Baal's footstool. He admitted "I cannot be king on Mount Zaphon." And instead he became an earthly king.

But Baal's loyal sister Anat was determined to bring her brother back to life. Her heart beating for him like a cow's heart for her calf, she went down a second time to Mot's realm and seized the dark lord by his cloak, screaming, "Give me back my brother!" But Mot replied, "What do you want of me, Anat? Yes, I swallow people up. I crunched the mighty Baal like a lamb in my jaws. That's how it is." At these words the enraged Anat took hold of Mot. She cut him with a blade, winnowed him with a winnowing fan, parched him with fire, ground him with a millstone and finally scattered him in the fields for the birds to eat.

It has been suggested that Anat's powerful and decisive action refers to the conclusion of the harvest, the preparation of corn for consumption, and its resowing the following season. But there are difficulties with this interpretation for the person who returned as new corn was not Mot, but Baal. There can be no doubt, however, that Anat had broken the grip of the dry season.

In anticipation of the return of the rains, the compassionate El had a dream in which he foresaw massed clouds raining oil and the dry watercourses running with honey – symbols of plenty. He awoke and cried out for joy: "My heart can rest tranquil in my breast! I know the mighty Baal is alive, the lord of the Earth! Shamash, goddess of the sun, go and look for shoots in the ploughed furrows! Is Baal visible yet?"

This fragment of a fresco, which decorated the palace walls in Mari, shows a bull being led to sacrifice. Baal's sister Anat and the sun goddess Shapash made animal sacrifices to the other gods on his behalf after they found his dead body.

Baal had indeed returned and all was well. But after seven years Mot reappeared before him, snarling, "It is because of you that I was cut, winnowed, parched, ground and scattered across the fields. If you do not give me one of your brothers, I shall consume the multitude on Earth!"

Mot and Baal faced each other, their eyes glowing like angry coals. Then they gored each other like wild bulls, they sank their teeth into each other like snakes, and they kicked each other like stallions. But the sun goddess Shamash called to Mot, "How dare you challenge the great Baal? Surely El will cast you down from your throne and break your sceptre." At this, Mot took fright and slunk away, leaving Baal to his throne.

The text ends here, but this battle was surely not the last. The nature of the conflict between Baal and Mot was cyclical and would repeat itself without end. Many of its features can be understood if it is interpreted in terms of the annual alternation of the rainy and dry seasons. Each year the rains, represented by Baal, faded away and their life-giving moisture trickled into the depths of the Earth, eventually disappearing. During the hot,

Anat, the Bloodthirsty Goddess

The goddess Anat, often identified with Astarte, is the local form of a deity who was recognized throughout the ancient Near East. Despite being associated with both sexual love and fertility, in one story she is the perpetrator of a frenzy of bloodshed which led to numerous deaths.

In an episode that can only be described as a digression in the Baal cycle, Anat indulges in two massacres.

The tale begins with Anat's extermination of the populations of two neighbouring cities. Raising her, scythe high above her, she stood astride a pile of severed human heads strewn like reaped corn. With mutilated hands flying around her, she wallowed up to her thighs in human blood.

Then she invited an army of soldiers to her palace and slaughtered them as they sat at her dinner table. After calmly rearranging the tables and chairs, she washed and purified herself in Baal's rain and dew.

Baal then spoke to Anat of the powers of his rain and its link to human sexuality. "Lay out delicious fruits of the Earth," he told her, "encourage marriages throughout the land, spread love over the Earth. Hasten to me and I shall tell you something of which the trees speak and the stones whisper, of which the heavens murmur to the Earth and the abyss murmurs to the stars. I know the secret of lightning, unknown to humankind."

This passage may refer to a "sacred marriage" or ritualized sexual union between Anat and Baal, which is described in explicit language in other, more fragmentary texts. It has also been suggested that the viscious massacres by the goddess represent a fertility sacrifice. However, the true interpretation of the story remains uncertain.

The cycle of myths about Baal and Mot may have represented the alternation between rainy and dry seasons. This scene of cultivation in Latakia, in modern Syria, reflects how from time immemorial, farmers of the region have worked the land to make the most of the fertility brought by the arrival of the rains.

dry summer, the gods in mourning "ploughed" their own flesh and sowed the new corn in readiness for the return of the rains in the autumn. The following spring, the rains faded away again.

It is quite possible that the myth was recited each year at an autumnal New Year festival and that the recitation was accompanied by a ritual enactment of the battle between Baal and Mot. As well as the annual cycle of the seasons, the myth also hints at another, longer process. The reappearance of Mot after seven years probably refers to the agricultural custom of allowing the fields to lie fallow every seventh, or "sabbatical" year. The story may reflect the cumulative impact of a succession of dry years, as described in the biblical reference to "seven lean years".

Aqhat, the Long-awaited Heir

This myth, like that of Keret (see pages 112–13), draws a parallel between the king's need for an heir and his ability to guarantee the fertility of his people's crops. The story shows a world in which gods and men are inextricably linked. They meet on common ground, and what happens on Earth is determined by events in the realm of the gods, which are in their turn influenced by the affairs of humans.

King Daniel was very unhappy. Although he had a fine daughter Pughat, he had no son to continue his line after him. So he decided to sleep in the temple, in the hope of receiving a dream bearing messages from the gods. Each day he made an offering to the entire pantheon and each evening he lay down to sleep. But every morning he would awake without having received any sign.

On the seventh day, Baal took pity on him. "Father El," he said, addressing the chief of the gods, "Daniel has no son to set up a memorial stone to his ancestors and to lay out funeral offerings. He has no one to protect his guests or to hold his hand when he is drunk. He has no one reliable to mend his roof or to wash his clothes. Every day he makes offerings to the gods. Can you not bless him with a son?" El was moved by these words, and replied, "Let his wife conceive a son, who will do all these things for him." Soon afterwards, to Daniel's delight, Aqhat was born.

King Ashurbanipal on a hunt, from the North Palace, Nineveh. Majesty was a fragile inheritance in the ancient Near East, always dependent on the production of a male successor.

On the seventh day after Aqhat's birth, Daniel looked up and saw the divine craftsman Kothar wa-Hasis approaching from Egypt. The king entertained his eminent guest with a feast and Kothar wa-Hasis presented Aqhat with a magnificent bow and arrows which he had made himself.

But the gift aroused the envy of the goddess Anat, who possibly thought that the weapons were destined for her. When Aqhat had grown up, Anat offered him as much gold and silver as he wished in exchange for them. But Aqhat refused to part with the weapons, and advised her to commission another set from Kothar wa-Hasis.

Anat persisted and made him a much greater offer. "If you give me the bow and arrows I will give you eternal life. You will live as long as Baal himself!" Aqhat was not deceived. In words which are strikingly similar to those of Gilgamesh when he rejected the sexual advances of Ishtar (see pages 82–83), he answered, "Don't lie to me! I know what happens to a mortal in the end ... I am sure to die. And anyway," he added as a final insult, "whoever heard of a woman hunting?"

Anat laughed in defiance. "You may reject my offer now, you gorgeous young man," she retorted, "but I shall grind you under my feet." Incensed by his rejection, she went immediately to her father El to seek permission to attack and humiliate Aqhat.

As before when she had petitioned him for Baal's palace (see page 102), she once again swore that she would beat El about the head until his grey beard ran with blood if he did not grant her what she wanted. El replied, "I know how angry you are. You'll do what you want anyway. Whoever insults you will be destroyed."

Anat laughed again and went to hire a drunken soldier called Yatpan to assist with Aqhat's murder. "Listen, Yatpan," she said, "Aqhat will be sitting down to eat and he will be all alone. While he is eating, a flock of vultures will be circling overhead. I'll be one of those vultures, and I'll carry you with me. As we pass over Aqhat's head, you must strike him twice on the skull and three times over the ear. His breath will depart from his nostrils like wind and vapour."

Everything went as planned. Carried over Aqhat as he was eating, Yatpan was able to reach down and strike him dead and retrieve the bow and arrows. But then something apparently went wrong.

At this point the text breaks off, but, according to one reading of the few surviving words, Yatpan dropped the bow into the water on the way back from his mission. According to another, Anat had not meant to kill Aqhat outright but only to stun him and later bring him back to consciousness. But sadly Anat could not persuade the powers of death to release him.

The goddess wept at the failure of her plan, perhaps out of pique at losing the bow but more probably out of regret for killing Aqhat. Outraged at Aqhat's death Baal caused the fruit and the corn to wither. Aqhat's sister Pughat sensed intuitively that something had happened to her brother and started mourning, while their father Daniel, unsure whose death had caused the drought, prayed for rain. The old king toured his fields on a donkey and kissed one withered stalk of corn after another with the words, "Dear stalk, if only you would grow, then my son Aqhat would harvest you and store you in the granary!"

No sooner had he uttered these words than two messengers came across the parched fields with the news of Aqhat's death. Daniel broke into a sweat and his body crumpled. He looked up at

With the help of a drunken soldier, Anat planned to kill Aqhat while he ate beneath circling vultures. She was irked because he had refused to give her his bow and arrows.

a group of vultures circling overhead and realized that they had been feasting on his son's corpse. "May Baal break your wings," he cursed them, "may you fall helpless to the ground!" Baal heard his call and responded by shattering the vultures' wings, causing them to fall at Daniel's feet. Daniel opened them up to look for the remains of his son, but the vultures' gizzards were empty. "May Baal restore your wings!" he prayed, and they came back to life and flew away.

A second time he looked up, and this time saw the father of the vultures overhead. Again he

This dagger with a gold blade and a handle ornately decorated with lapis lazuli and golden studs comes from the Royal Cemetery of Ur. Disguising herself as the goddess Anat, Pughat armed herself with a dagger in order to kill her brother's murderer.

asked Baal to shatter the vulture's wings so that it would drop to Earth. Once more he searched the gizzards, but this vulture too was empty and he asked Baal to let it fly away.

A third time he looked up, and this time saw the mother of the vultures. She too fell to Earth and when Daniel cut her open he found the fat and bones of his son. He wept as he buried them and prolonged his mourning for seven years while the god Baal continued to withhold his life-giving rains so that the world suffered.

When the time prescribed for grief was finally over, Aqhat's sister Pughat decided on an act of revenge. She asked her father's blessing for a mission to find her brother's murderer and kill him in turn. Daniel answered, "Pughat, carrier of water, who brushes the early dew from the barley, who knows the course of the stars, may you kill the man who killed your brother, may you destroy the man who destroyed the heir of your family."

Carefully disguising herself as the goddess Anat, Pughat thereupon hid a dagger under her dress and went to where the thug Yatpan was lounging in his tent. Yatpan was already drinking and offered her wine, boasting, "The hand that killed Aqhat can kill a thousand enemies."

The remainder of the story is lost, but the text breaks off on a sinister note: "Twice she gave him wine to drink ... " The most likely conclusion is that Pughat made Yatpan drunk and then killed him in his stupor. It is also likely that this deed put an end to the drought and somehow brought Aqhat back to life to continue Daniel's lineage.

Brother, Sister and Lover

Baal's sister Anat was one of several similar Near Eastern goddesses of fertility, sex and violence: Ishtar, Astarte and Inana. But Anat and her Egyptian counterpart, Isis, were very different from these other goddesses in at least one important way. They both became the lovers of their own brothers and later bore children from the union.

Incestuous unions between gods may have been used to justify similar arrangements in the royal households. In Egypt, it was certainly the custom for the pharaoh to marry his sister as a way of ensuring that the royal bloodline remained unsullied. Clearly the people of Canaan must have been influenced by the ideas of their Egyptian neighbours, but much less is known about Ugaritic society, so it is impossible to say for sure whether incest was sanctioned by tradition.

Several fragmentary texts refer to the erotic relationship between brother and sister, Anat and Baal (see page 106). The virginity of Anat was obviously considered important as a great deal of emphasis is put on it in both texts.

The remains of one text tell of the time when Anat went in search of Baal, who was out hunting. Baal saw his sister approaching. "He lifted up his eyes and looked, looked on the virgin Anat, most gracious among the sisters of Baal."

Baal was not shy about his desire, nor about his success as a lover, so he proudly cried: "Now shalt thou be exalted! For Baal will anoint the horn of thy prowess, virgin Anat. Baal will anoint the horn of thy prowess."

The text then goes on to describe how Anat gave birth to Baal's child. "She went and went away all alone to the pleasant and fair places. She bore a steer for Baal."

Anat was often a bloodthirsty goddess, but her affection for her brother never faded, even when he was dead. Another fragment tells of Anat's love for Baal after his death. "A day, two days passed, and the damsel Anat sought him. Like the desire of the heart of a heifer for her calf, like that of the heart of an ewe for her lamb, so is the desire of the heart of Anat."

This haunting image of the Syrian goddess Ashtart, who had some of the same characteristics as the Ugaritic goddess Anat, conveys a sense of both her power and sexuality (*c.*600BC).

A King's Tribulations

A king's need for an heir recurs in this story about the monarch of Hubur. However, the myth of King Keret explores the problems of the successful transmission of power well beyond the initial question of childlessness.

Keret, king of the city of Hubur, was in despair. Once the head of a mighty dynasty, with numerous brothers and sons, he was now left alone without heirs. Every one of his children had died, some of disease, some in childbirth, others at sea or in battle. Even his wife had abandoned him.

Keret shut himself up in his room, weeping tears until sleep at last overpowered him. The god El appeared to him in a dream and asked him, "Keret, are you weeping because you want more power and wealth?" But Keret answered, "What use to me are mines of silver and gold and stables full of horses? I need sons!"

The compassionate El replied, "Cease your weeping, Keret. Get up, wash and purify yourself." He ordered the king to make sacrifices to himself and Baal and to lead an army against against King Pabil of Udum. "Let your vast army advance like locusts for seven days towards the city of Udum. Besiege the city – after seven days, King Pabil will be unable to sleep for the neighing of his horses, the lowing of his oxen and the howling of his dogs. Then he will send messengers to you, offering gifts. Do not accept them; ask instead for the hand of his lovely daughter Hurriya, beautiful as the goddess Anat. Tell him that El granted this to you in a dream. She will bear you sons."

Keret awoke and hastened to obey the god's words. On the third day of the army's expedition, the soldiers passed the cities of Tyre and Sidon where Keret sought the support of the local goddess Athirat. "If I succeed with your help in bringing the beautiful Hurriya to my house," he vowed, "I shall repay you in gold and silver."

Having made this promise, Keret left Tyre and Sidon behind and arrived at Udum on the seventh day. By the seventh night of the siege, King Pabil was unable to sleep and sent a messenger to Keret offering him riches, just as El had foretold. Keret asked only for the hand of his daughter Hurriya. On hearing this request, Pabil was very sad but he was compelled to let his daughter go.

El was pleased with the fulfilment of his plan and for seven years blessed Keret with sons and daughters. But in his happiness Keret forgot his vow to Athirat. Now she prepared to call him to account. She cursed him so that he fell gravely ill, which in turn caused Baal to withhold his rain, and that led to famine.

Keret's son Ilihu wept, saying, "My father, how can you not be immortal, how can you just die like a dog?" Keret told his son, "Do not grieve, but instruct your loving sister to lament for me and to prepare my grave." Meanwhile El was moved by compassion for Keret and asked the assembly of the gods if anyone was capable of defeating Keret's disease. Seven times he asked, but each time he received no answer. Finally, El decided to heal Keret himself and to this end he created Shataqat, goddess of healing.

Shataqat flew into Keret's chamber, where she wiped away the sweat of his fever and restored his appetite, breaking Athirat's curse. Immediately Keret called for a lamb to be cooked and ate heartily. But his eldest son Yassib, goaded by an inner demon, came to him, saying, "Father, you have become weak, you are unfit to discharge the duties of a king. Let me be king." But with his strength restored Keret was not ready to abdicate and instead cursed his son with an early death.

The text breaks off in mid-sentence, but there may be clues to the story's ending in the Old Testament tale of David, which likewise explores the difficulty of sustaining a king's effectiveness: as David became senile, his sons Adonijah and Solomon fought for the throne (I Kings 1–2).

Following the advice of El, father of the gods, King Keret besieges the city of Udum until the unceasing noise of animals starving drives its citizens to surrender.

THE HITTITES

"Up then! Let us fight, and let the proud storm god, my lord, decide our case!" Such was the challenge hurled at a neighbouring monarch by King Mursilis II in the fourteenth century BC. As so often at this time, the mighty storm god Teshub favoured his own Hittite forces: the armies of Arzawa were smashed – their city was sacked. Its smouldering ruins were given over for grazing to Teshub's two bulls, Seris and Hurris, as the Hittites added another province to their realm.

Thundering across the heavens in his vast, bull-drawn chariot, brandishing an axe in one hand and a jagged lightning bolt in the other, the all-conquering Teshub made a fitting figurehead for the brave, warlike people who, for several centuries in the second millennium BC, held much of Asia Minor in their sway. They extended their empire through modern Turkey into Syria, Lebanon and Palestine, reaching Babylon and for a time even rivalling the pharaohs in Egypt.

A great military and commercial power, the Hittites were one of the most influential peoples of the ancient world, yet their origins are mysterious. Their name comes from the land of Hatti, the wild region of Anatolia which was their heartland. However, the Hittites were not native to this area. They were the descendants of a nameless group of Indo-European invaders who left a homeland somewhere beyond the Black Sea and arrived in Asia Minor between the fifth and third millennia.

Just as the Hittites seemed content with inheriting the name of their adoptive homeland, so they took a relaxed attitude to the religion and mythology of their growing state. Rather than imposing an ancestral religion upon their new subjects, the Hittite rulers assimilated deities and myths from the various different parts of their kingdom into a single state creed. In this official religion, the king served not merely as monarch but as high priest making a progress each year through the scattered shrines of his far-flung realm, presiding at the most important local festivals. Where other conquerors may have confronted insubordinate satellites, the Hittite rulers fostered a sense of belonging, reinforced by a shared mythology that gave their state a common identity and purpose.

Left: **This silver and gold-leaf statuette of a mother goddess (*c.*2000BC) is believed to have come from a grave near Ankara, Turkey. It is only 20cm high.**

Opposite: **King Warpalawas pays homage to an unknown god in this neo-Hittite relief (*c.*800BC). As the leader of a great military nation the Hittite king played an important role in maintaining his country's reputation.**

Land of a Thousand Gods

In the ethnic crucible of the Hittite kingdom dozens of disparate peoples and a score of separate cities were combined to form a single nation. This diverse civic structure was matched by a varied collection of gods. As the empire expanded, the pantheon altered dramatically. New deities were added, old ones discarded, and some were even merged. In this way, the list of Hittite gods grew in response to the evolving needs of the state.

The Hittites called their pantheon "The Thousand Gods", and it was not an inappropriate name. Every city, every mountain, and even every spring seems to have had its own particular deity, while there were others to govern the passage of the seasons, the growth of the crops, and the fortunes of the local community in peace and in war. The Hittite state tolerated local differences and inspired contentment and loyalty by respecting the diversity of its people. For the kingdom to feel truly united, however, a common national religion was required with a pantheon of key gods and goddesses that could be recognized across the whole kingdom.

During the fifteenth century BC, the war-weakened rulers of the Old Hittite kingdom were challenged and conquered by a new dynasty of rulers from the north-western Mesopotamian kingdoms of Mittani and Hurri, southeast of the Hittite empire. The new Hittite rulers, however, proved as flexible as ever in adapting to these changing circumstances. Often Hurrian names and identities were simply grafted on to older deities already assimilated into Hittite religion from an earlier faith. So it was that the head of the spiritual hierarchy, the Hattian weather god Taru, acquired a new title as Teshub, angry storm god of the Hittites. Teshub was held in great awe; he presented a terrifying prospect in his chariot drawn by his bulls, ready to smash the petty endeavours and aspirations of humankind.

This preoccupation with the weather unites the Hittites with other peoples of the ancient Near East. In Mesopotamia's fertile plains, the sun and rivers may have seemed faithful friends; but in Anatolia's rugged mountains a storm could destroy a year's harvest in a single night, and the blazing sun during a period of drought could easily burn an entire crop. In such a capricious climate the sense of impending disaster and threat to humanity could never be entirely banished.

A fearsome god, to be appeased at all costs, Teshub was proud, potent and unpredictable. He had ascended his throne in a violent coup against his father, Kumarbi, and dispossessed an entire generation of deities in the process. The usurped generation included the old sea god whose name is now unknown, and Ubelluri, who bore the whole Earth on his shoulder. Other dark primeval deities associated with the Earth and the Underworld such as Hannahanna, the ancient mother goddess, were neutral in the struggle.

The storm god's queen, Hebat, was as majestic as the lion on whose back she calmly stood. As the Hittite Empire was established she replaced the sun goddess Wurusemu, whose shrine was at Arinna, a city one day's journey south of the Hittite capital Hattusas. Given a new Hurrian name and reinvented as Teshub's consort, she became the first lady of the official Hittite pantheon. Their son, Sharruma, referred to traditionally as "the calf of Teshub", inherited his father's association with the bull. The storm god's sister, Sauska, shared her brother's warlike spirit. Her identity also merged over time with that of her Hurrian equivalent, Ishtar, and she was numbered among the most important Hittite deities.

Another old Hurrian deity named as one of Teshub's nearest henchmen was Simige, the sun god. He took on the role and attributes of the Hattian sun god Estan, just as Kattahziwuri, the Hattian goddess who dominated the Hittite world of magic, was syncretized with her Hurrian equivalent, a goddess called Kamrusepa.

"My son is great: he ploughs and harrows; he waters the fields and brings forth the crops." So said the old Hattian storm god Taru speaking of Telipinu, his son by the sun goddess Wurusemu. Perhaps because his role as god of agriculture was central to the continuation of life, Telipinu retained both his name and his identity during the merging of Hurrian and Hattian deities.

Although the Mesopotamian's great achievements had made their culture dominant throughout the ancient Near East, the Hittites stayed relatively free of southern influences. Nonetheless, as their god of wisdom they adopted the cunning Ea (Enki), the Mesopotamian god associated with the vast freshwater sea said to lie beneath the Earth.

Modern-day Boghazkoy in Turkey was once the site of Hattusas, capital of the Hittite Empire. The city gained its status during the reign of the Hittite king, Labarnas I, *c.*1680BC.

The Storm God and the Serpent

Two myths describe the conflicts between Teshub and a fearsome serpent called Illuyanka. Both present the most powerful of the gods as vulnerable. Teshub sustains severe injuries himself and is even, for a time, unable to protect his people from evil and famine.

Despite Teshub's all-conquering image and his position in the pantheon as an immortal military leader, one of the Hittites' most memorable myths begins not with one of his victories but with his defeat by the Earth serpent Illuyanka. The story exists in two different versions, each of which opens with the declaration that Teshub and the serpent fought and that the god was badly injured.

For the ancient Anatolians from whom the Hittites inherited this myth, the serpent was a symbol of evil. Illuyanka's victory over Teshub represented the catastrophe of a poor spring and its effect on the population. As the god of war and weather, Teshub protected his people both from enemy armies and the extremes of the elements; his failure to assure clement conditions was comparable to the disaster of military defeat.

In the first version of this tale, Teshub, unsure about how he should overcome the humiliation of failure, called upon his fellow deities for advice and assistance. His daughter, Inara, responded immediately and prepared a vast banquet with an abundance of delicious food and huge vats of wine and beer. Then she enlisted the help of a mortal man, Hupasiya, in her enterprise. Hupasiya agreed to assist her on condition that she slept with him first. Inara did so, then returned with him to the hall where the banquet awaited them. Hiding Hupasiya, she called Illuyanka up from his hole in the ground: "I have prepared you a feast," she said, "come and help yourself." The serpent ascended with all his children, and they fell greedily upon the assembled delicacies. Bloated and drowsy from over-indulgence, they could no longer get back into their hole in the ground. Hupasiya easily

The god of storms Teshub is depicted wielding lightning and an axe in this 9th-century BC basalt relief. As well as storms, Teshub presided over battles and offered divine protection to the Hittite people against their enemies.

tied up Illuyanka, whereupon Teshub was able to come and kill him.

As a reward for Hupasiya's help, Inara built him a house on an isolated clifftop where they lived together as lovers. But one day, Inara had to go on a long journey, leaving her mortal lover at home by himself. "Whatever you do," she warned him, "don't look out of the window. For if you do you will see your estranged wife and children." Beautiful and powerful as she was, Inara knew that her hold upon Hupasiya could not match that of his mortal wife and family. He obeyed her dutifully for twenty days, but finally his patience was exhausted: he pushed open the window and looked out. As Inara predicted, there were his wife and children. From that moment onward had everything changed. As soon as the goddess returned from her journey her lover began to complain, pleading to be allowed to return home to his family. Her reaction is unknown as the tablet on which this version of the myth is recorded breaks off at this point, but it seems likely that Hupasiya was punished for his disobedience.

In the other version of the story, Illuyanka not only defeats Teshub but manages to rob him of his heart and his eyes. The storm god himself devises a cunning strategy for getting them back, and finally triumphs over the serpent.

The Celebrations of Spring

"Let the land thrive and be fertile, and may it be protected!" bids Kella, Teshub's priest in one version of the Illuyanka myth. The annual regeneration of the crops was an event celebrated in the Hittites' greatest festival.

Each spring, the new year was marked by the Purulli festival, a grand religious ceremony at the climax of which the Illuyanka myth was recited or perhaps acted out. So crucial was this feast in the Hittite year that King Mursilis II is reported to have once returned from a military campaign abroad so that he could be at home in Hattusas for the festivities.

The myth of Teshub's initial defeat followed by his eventual victory shows how the nation survived off the land according to the vagaries of nature.

The temporary suspension of the storm god's benevolent rule suggests the sterile stagnation of winter – a potentially permanent condition, it is implied, were it not for the god's annual struggle. After centuries of farming the unyielding soil of mountainous Anatolia, the Hittites knew better than to take nature and its unpredictable rhythms for granted. Each spring was cause for celebration, as it heralded a victory over the enemies of life.

Purulli triumphantly feted this renewal – its name actually means "of the Earth".

A Hittite stone relief depicts revellers at a feast. Each year the arrival of spring was a cause for celebration.

The Earth Abandoned

In those stories that tell of disappearing gods, Hittite mythology returned again and again to a nightmarish vision of a world devoid of auspicious elemental conditions. In these tales crops lay withered in barren fields, once healthy livestock bellowed in hunger and pain, and humankind was forsaken by its divine protectors.

The Hittites were haunted by the fear that one day nature might abandon their land, causing hardship and eventual extinction. Nowhere is this preoccupation more apparent than in myths that describe the disappearance of powerful deities. In these unsettling tales, largely inherited from the mythology of the Hittites' Anatolian adoptive homeland, the deities that normally protected the Earth and humankind vanish, leaving the land infertile and the people impoverished and hungry.

A mother goddess gives birth between two protective leopards in this terracotta sculpture from Chatal Huyuk in southern Anatolia (c.6000–5800BC).

One of the most dramatic of these stories tells of the disappearance of the Sun God. Resenting the Teshub's rule, the ancient Sea God was in rebellious mood. He resolved to attack the Earth by abducting the sun, which gave heat and light. "If I seize the Sun God and hide him away," he reasoned, "what can the storm god do?"

One evening, at the end of the sun's daily transit across the heavens, the Sea God trapped the Sun God in a net and imprisoned him in a giant jar. In the sun's absence, Frost dominated the land. Seed lay infertile in the bare Earth, sheep and cattle fell dead in withered fields, and their mortal masters died in their thousands as famine besieged the world. Shocked by what he saw, Teshub was unable to find a way out of this desperate situation. The land, it appeared, was quite dead. "When a man has died," he implored, "can they bring him back to life? If an ox or sheep has been killed, can that be brought back to life?"

What miracle, then, could restore the Earth to life? It seemed to Teshub as if there was no power left that could save the world – not even his own. He sent his supporters in search of the Sun God, but to no avail. His son Telipinu also set out to rescue the sun, only to be seized and imprisoned himself. The great mother goddess, Hannahanna herself, attempted to find the sun too, but she returned defeated. One by one the gods went to do battle with Frost and one by one they were humiliated or taken prisoner. Teshub was stunned into helplessness. "Frost has paralyzed the entire land," he acknowledged. "He has even frozen the waters. Frost is all-powerful."

Although the clay tablet bearing this story almost completely disintegrates at this point, a

Telipinu and the Sea God's Daughter

The disappearance of the Sun God is a common theme in the Hittite myths. In this particular tale, the mighty deity is dragged from his rightful place in the sky, down to the depths of the ocean. His absence creates devastation on land. Crops fail and famine causes hardship for animals and humankind alike.

One day, the Sea God found himself quarrelling with the Sun God. Mighty in his wrath, the Sea God attacked the very Heavens, dragging his rival from the sky to hide him away in the ocean depths. With the sun's disappearance, the land was plunged into darkness and deprived of essential warmth. This caused the crops to fail, and famine and hardship reigned. But because no one could match the might of the Sea God, nothing, it seemed, could be done.

Presiding over a world in despair caused great concern to Teshub. He called to Telipinu, first and most favoured of his sons. "Telipinu, you must go to the sea where you will find the Sun God. Bring him back so that we can return him to the sky." Telipinu obeyed his father and journeyed to the sea. Seeing the young god draw near, the Sea God grew afraid, and offered Telipinu his daughter in marriage, before handing over the kidnapped Sun God.

Telipinu returned to the Earth with his bride, and positioned the Sun God in the sky. Life flourished again in the world; with the sun's light and warmth, the crops grew again, livestock bred and humankind thrived.

But that was not the end of the episode. The Sea God sent a river with a message to Teshub: "Your son Telipinu took my daughter away with him as his wife. What bride-price are you going to pay me?" The Sea God was persistent and so Teshub turned to the mother goddess Hannahanna for advice. "The Sea God keeps demanding his bride-price," he told her. "Should I give it to him?" Hannahanna's response was clear:
"Of course," she said. "Telipinu took his daughter, the Sea God is entitled to his payment." So Teshub gave the Sea God a thousand cattle and a thousand sheep, and thus harmony was restored.

Overwhelmed with anger the Sea God attacks the Sun God, wrenching him from the sky and keeping him captive in the ocean.

few concluding lines survive suggesting that a sacrifice was made as ransom for the Sun God. Such sacrifices, according to the myth, should be practised by all: "If you, O Sun God, grant your help to a man, let that man sacrifice to you nine animals. If he is poor, he need only give you a single sheep."

The most complete extant myth describing the loss of a god is that which features Teshub's favourite son, Telipinu, the all-important god of agriculture. The three slightly different versions of this story all agree on its main points. Telipinu strode off in anger one day because his worshippers had neglected their duties. According to the myth, as a token of his wrath and the threat of disorder that it posed for the world, "he put his right shoe on his left foot, and the left on the right". The results were immediate and dramatic: "Mist enveloped the windows. Fog blanketed the house ... The gods on their altars were suffocated. The sheep were stifled in their pens ... The ewe rejected her lamb, and the cow repelled her calf." Animals that were already pregnant were unable to give birth. Gods and humanity were alike affected.

In trepidation, Teshub sent an eagle to find his missing son. "Go and search the high mountains," he said. "Seek in the valleys and the deep blue of the sea." But the eagle returned having sought in vain. Teshub then decided to hunt for his son himself, but he too was unsuccessful. Finally, the Mother Goddess Hannahanna sent a bee to look for Telipinu. When Teshub heard of her plan he was sceptical: "When gods great and small have failed to find my son, how is this bee going to help? His wings are small; and he himself is tiny ... " But Teshub was underestimating a creature whose poisonous sting was regarded in folk medicine as potent enough to be a cure for severe paralysis. Added to which, the bees' precious honey was revered throughout the ancient world as a powerful purifying agent and it was even thought to drive away evil spirits.

Hittite myths express the fears of a people exposed to harsh weather conditions and hardship caused by drought. Scenes such as this arid landscape in the Hittite area of modern-day Turkey must have haunted the popular imagination.

The bee eventually found the agriculture god asleep in a hiding place, and used his powerful sting to awaken him. This only added to Telipinu's anger, and he raged through the world once more, leaving a trail of devastation behind him. Only the sacrifices and spells of the goddess of magic, Kamrusepa, could placate him. She burned brushwood over his body so that his wrath might likewise burn up. Then, she extinguished the fire, so that his fury might be extinguished in the process. She made an offering of malt – considered useless for seed or for flour – so that his anger might become futile.

Eventually, Kamrusepa was able to return with a positive report for the other gods, who were waiting in convocation under a hawthorn tree: "I have drained the evil from Telipinu's body. I have taken his wrath. I have purged his sin." Telipinu returned home in peace, borne on the back of an eagle, and took charge of his land. Giving it his protection once more, he nurtured the Earth, filling it with every kind of abundance.

Kumarbi, Father of the Gods

The Hittites placed the war between the generations at the very centre of history. Their stories tell of the gods negotiating the persistent jealousies of family life and tackle the question of the mysterious origins of the principles by which the world is governed.

A group of myths now known as the "Kumarbi Cycle" was drawn from Hurrian mythology. In them the storm god Teshub was held to have seized the throne of the kingdom of Heaven from his own father, Kumarbi. Yet Kumarbi himself had been a usurper. Containing some of the most important Hittite stories, this epic sequence tells of the mysterious origins of the world, and of the battles for supremacy between the primeval deities.

The Kumarbi cycle is also important in establishing some of the criteria which the Hittites used to formulate their notion of the universe, highlighting as it does the developing oppositions between Earth, darkness and the past (represented by Kumarbi), and sky, light and the present (all the province of Teshub). It is significant that Ea, god of wisdom, is seen gradually to shift his allegiance in the course of the cycle, from father to son, from old regime to new, and from the past to the future.

"Let the great gods listen!" begins the Song of Kumarbi, the opening story of the cycle. "Long ago, in primeval times, Alalu was the king of Heaven." As Alalu sat on his throne, his courtier, Anu, led the other gods in obeisance, bowing down at the ruler's feet, and waiting on him attentively by constantly filling his drinking cup. Alalu, however, was to benefit from only nine year of such treatment: at the end of that time, his subjects turned against him. The unseated ruler fled from the rebels to the depths of the Earth, while Anu replaced him as king in Heaven.

The gods were now led in homage by Kumarbi who similarly knelt before the new king and attended to his every wish. When nine years had passed, however, he too rebelled. Knowing that he was no match in combat for Kumarbi, Anu sought safety in flight. But Kumarbi caught him by the legs and brought him tumbling down from the sky. Biting at Anu's loins, Kumarbi severed his enemy's genitals, swallowing them whole. He was secure now, he gloated, not only from Anu but from any potential heir of his. But the fallen king warned him against false triumph. Along with his male member, Anu explained, Kumarbi had swallowed his sperm and was consequently pregnant with the offspring of the storm god Teshub, his vizier Tasmisu and the mighty River Tigris.

At this stage the clay tablet on which the story has survived becomes fragmentary, leaving confusion

Kumarbi's subjects made a show of their devotion by keeping his drinking cup full. This example in silver dates from c.1400–1200BC.

The Battle of Generations

Kumarbi's castration of his predecessor, Anu, echoes Kronos's attack on his father Uranus in Greek mythology. After their conflict, Uranus's genitals fall into the sea, and giants, nymphs and the Furies emerge from the bloodied foam just as Teshub, Tasmisu and the River Tigris spring from the seed of Anu's severed genitals that were consumed by his son.

The Greek god Kronos had six children by his wife Rhea, all of which he tried to eat. His jealous hostility towards his own offspring set in train a generation war between the older Titans and the younger Olympian deities.

In the Greek myth, as in the Hittite, this familial conflict resulted in the transfer of power from an Earth god (Kumarbi, Kronos) to a deity of the air (Teshub, the storm god, or Zeus, the god of the sky). Such similarities shared by the two cultures are too great to be dismissed as coincidence. Both tales, it seems certain, must be versions of an ancient Hurrian myth. One was inherited by the Hittites, the other – carried across the Aegean from the later Anatolian colonies – would one day re-emerge in the mythology of classical Greece.

The River Tigris, shown here, was said in myth to have been created during a conflict between the gods Anu and Kumarbi.

as to how the narrative concluded. According to one interpretation, King Kumarbi spat out Anu's sperm only to impregnate the Earth itself with Anu's great progeny. In another, the terrible seed continued to grow in Kumarbi's belly, to be delivered at the allotted time. Either way, the gods were born. Kumarbi called upon the god of wisdom, Ea, for help in his conflict with Teshub, but no force in Heaven or on Earth could check the wild storm god. "Who can match me in battle?" asked Teshub, "Who can prevail against me now?"

The remainder of the Kumarbi Cycle concerns his repeated attempts to overthrow his rebellious offspring. Rather than claim the crown and its power for himself, however, he decided to put forward a series of rival pretenders in his place. The first of these was a bold, fearless young god whose name is unknown. He took his bow, and attacked Teshub with a hail of arrows. The first struck the storm god's sister, Sauska. As the second arrow whizzed by him, Teshub pulled the wounded Sauska into his chariot and made ready to charge, but the young god's third arrow halted the vehicle. Then Teshub's opponent hurled a stone, which struck the sky and brought his enemy tumbling ignominiously to Earth, followed closely by his chariot. The young god seized the reins, wrenching the whip from the storm god's helpless hand. "Those are sacred reins," protested Teshub. But his rival defied him, proclaiming that Teshub's chariot was now his. Teshub was king no longer, the triumphant young god declared; he was master himself and he intended to rule the Heavens.

For some years the young nameless god ruled unchallenged, but in time he became complacent. When the ancient goddess Kubaba bade him do honour to his divine ancestors, he scornfully refused, and instead congratulated himself on his own superiority. "They are great," he acknowledged, "but they do not intimidate me. I am their king." But his words came to Ea on the winds, and he was greatly angered.

"Something must be done about this king of ours," he said to Kumarbi. Ea dispatched an envoy to warn the young god but he simply insulted the messenger.

Infuriated, Ea ordered his emissary to go down to the Underworld where his brother Nara-Napsara reigned, and ask for his help. Ea's plea was not in vain. Calling together all the animals of the Earth, Nara-Napsara told them of the young god's intolerable disrespect for the rest of the pantheon. "Tear him! Trample him! Flay him!" he commanded. The animals obeyed and the young god was not only badly wounded – his pride was also shattered by the wild beasts' onslaught. Teshub returned, and cast him from his throne. The humiliated god hailed him in abject homage.

Silver, Son of the Storm God

The next candidate to test the storm god was Silver, Kumarbi's son by a mortal woman. He was a personification of the precious metal, revered by the Hittites for its properties and used by them as a currency. Silver was nonetheless unacknowledged by his father with the result that, though as great as any god in the pantheon, he was disregarded by worshippers, and had no cult of his own.

Growing up with his mother in the city like any other boy, Silver one day quarrelled with some orphans in the street outside his house. As the dispute became a fight, Silver struck at them with a stick. One of his opponents challenged him: "Who are you to hit us?" he asked. "You are an orphan, just like us!" Crying in humiliation, Silver ran to his mother and asked her what the other boy had meant. When she refused to answer, he threatened her in turn with his stick. "Your father is Kumarbi," she finally admitted, "and he lives in the city of Urkis. Your brother is Teshub, king of Heaven and Earth, and your sister is Sauska."

Without further ado, Silver left his home and his mother and started out for Urkis. On reaching the city, he found his father's house, but Kumarbi was not at home. Undaunted by this setback, Silver set off to find

Under orders from Ea, god of water, all the animals of the Earth attack the rebellious young god who usurped Teshub and refused to pay homage to his ancestors.

Men of Iron

Ubelluri's account of how an ancient copper-cutting tool was used to divide the Earth from the sky is testimony to the extravagance of the mythical imagination. It also highlights the significance of metalworking for the Hittites.

The Anatolian mountains are rich in minerals, and copper in particular had been a mainstay of the Hattian economy from the earliest times. The Hittites were renowned throughout the ancient world for their metalworking skills: already notable coppersmiths, they learned early to mix it with tin to make bronze. The Hittites also pioneered the systematic use of iron and the closely-guarded secret of its smelting gave them an advantage over enemies. Slag heaps found at the site of Hattusas, the Hittite capital, have proved the most enduring monuments to an industry that awed the ancient world.

This ornate circular standard (c.2600–1900BC) is characteristic of a society famous for its metalworking.

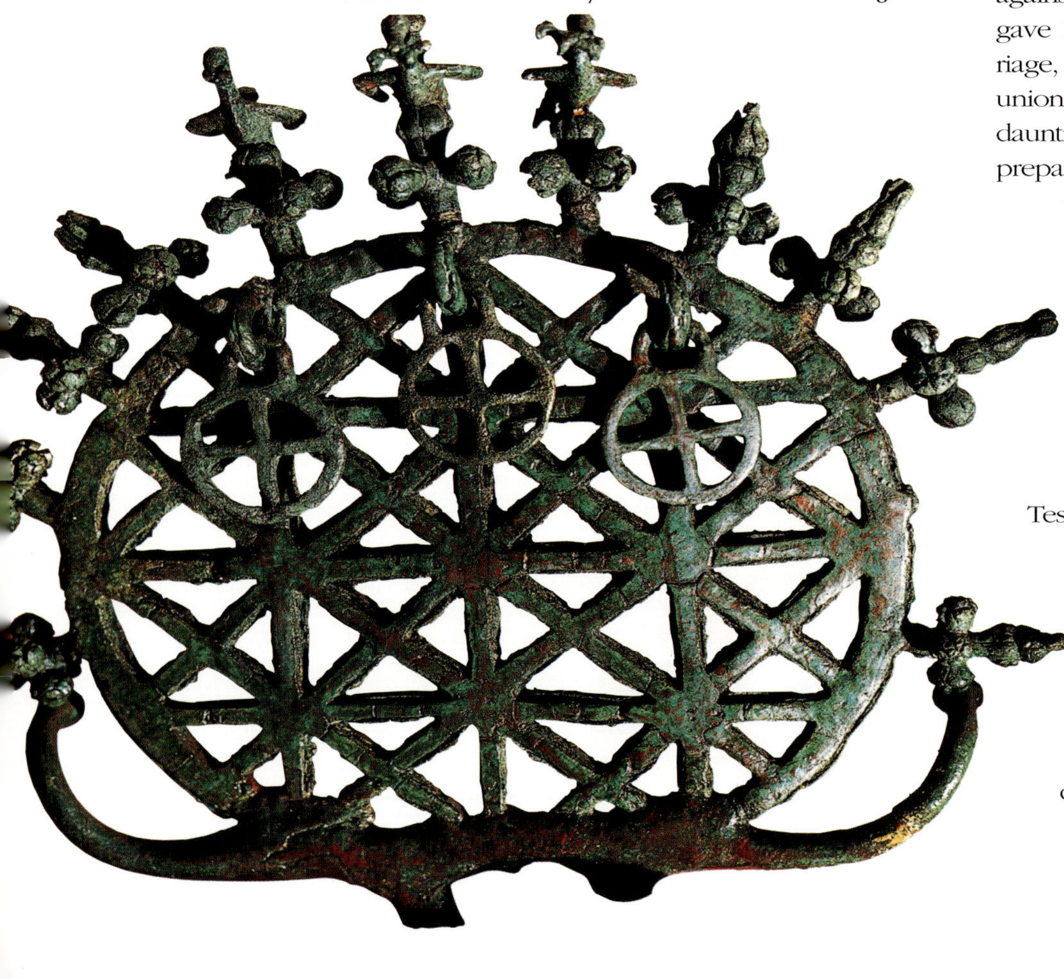

him, searching far and wide over mountains and plains. At this point, the clay tablet becomes difficult to read and the rest of the story is lost. It appears, however, that Silver finally tracked down the father who had abandoned him.

With his supplanter Teshub still on the throne, Kumarbi was at last prepared to acknowledge this lost son of his. Silver succeeded in toppling Teshub and seized the throne for himself.

The next recorded episode describes Teshub nursing his wounds after defeat, and being chided by his brother Tasmisu for his cowardice. "Where is your thunder now?" asks Tasmisu. "Silver controls all before him. Are you going to leave him in command?" But Silver, it seems, was unstoppable. In the next fragment of the tale we find him pulling the Sun and Moon down from the heavens, despite their pleas for mercy. "We give light to Heaven and Earth," they protest. "If you kill us, you will rule in darkness."

Yet Silver, in his turn, must have been brought down, for according to the next surviving fragment of the cycle, Kumarbi now appealed to the Sea God for help against another usurping son. In response, the Sea God gave Kumarbi his giant daughter Sertapsuruhi in marriage, and the sea serpent Hedammu was born of their union. A vast and powerful monster, Hedammu posed a daunting threat to Teshub. Yet even as the storm god was preparing himself for a duel to the death, his sister Sauska was plotting to overcome the serpent with cunning. Having bathed her lovely body and generously anointed herself with fragrant oils, she met the monster as he surfaced from the deep. "What woman is this?" asked Hedammu, enraptured as she approached him. Sauska offered him a love potion that was in reality a powerful sleeping draught. Hedammu was thus easily overpowered and Teshub's throne was secure again.

The Earth Monster

Deaf and blind as he was, the Earth monster Ullikummi was not so easily seduced and he posed a serious threat to Teshub. The offspring of Kumarbi and the personification of a mountain, Ullikummi was taken down to the Underworld after birth and placed on

Teshub's consort Queen Hebat stands astride a lion in this 1st-millennium BC stone relief. The couple remained foremost among the Hittite deities despite constant threats to the throne.

the shoulder of Ubelluri, the god on whose broad back both Heaven and Earth were supported. There, Kumarbi reasoned, the child would be safe from Sauska's prying eyes, and would grow up to oust Teshub.

After only fifteen days, however, Ullikummi's huge basalt body had broken through the surface of the sea and towered above the waves. With his thunder and rain massed behind, Teshub prepared to confront the giant. He tried every available tactic yet he failed to hinder the monster's inexorable advance. As Ullikummi arrived at the walls of the heavenly city, his sheer size persuaded Teshub to step down from his throne without a fight.

Exasperated at the instability and disquiet caused by Kumarbi's persistent attacks on the heavenly throne, his onetime ally Ea intervened on behalf of Teshub. Visiting Ubelluri to discuss what had happened, Ea was surprised to find that the god who held up the Heavens was unaware that Kumarbi had placed a monster on his shoulder. Ubelluri admitted that he could feel some pain there which reminded him of the day when the primeval gods had divided the Heavens from the Earth using an ancient copper chisel that cut stone. He had not been fully aware of his circumstances then, either. Ea was inspired and suggested a plan: they could use the chisel once more to cut away Ullikummi's basalt feet. The episode is incomplete, but it has been suggested that Ullikummi was thus disabled, and Teshub's supremacy was finally assured.

Legends of Gods and Men

Absorbed as they were with their own heavenly power struggles, the Hittite gods still found time to interest themselves in the affairs and the tribulations of ordinary, earthbound men and women. Such divine intervention in human society gave rise to some of the Hittites' most revealing and appealing myths.

The city of Kanesh (modern-day Kultepe) features in a series of Hittite stories about humankind and its fortunes. Archaeologists have discovered clay tablets from the ruins at Kanesh which locate the city at the centre of an extensive trading network.

Some of the Hittites' most interesting myths focus not on the cataclysmic conflicts of the gods but on the earthly history of humanity. The story of two real historical cities, Kanesh and Zalpa, is typical. It is contained on a fragmentary clay tablet and, as with so many Hittite stories, the narrative ends abruptly, leaving its outcome uncertain. While the remaining narrative has a serious message about the incest taboo, the story's significance lies more in its yoking together of two very different and distant cities. One was a remote mountain stronghold far inland, the other a bustling seaport – Kanesh and Zalpa might have appeared to have no similarities at all. But despite the geographical divide and for all their independence of spirit, a single kingdom and culture united the two disparate centres. As their citizens would be reminded each time they remembered this myth, the cities were linked to one another by a common Hittite heritage.

"The Queen of Kanesh once bore thirty sons at one time," the tale begins. "What a crowd I have produced!" she cried. Lining baskets with dung to make them watertight, she placed all her sons inside them, put the baskets in the river and sent them floating downstream. The current carried the babies all the way down the Red River to Zalpa on the coast. Here, the babies were spotted by the gods, who rescued them still alive from their frail coracles. They were taken ashore and brought up by the gods as their own.

Some years later, the Queen gave birth again, this time to thirty baby girls. These she kept with her, raising them herself as a devoted mother. By now, however, her sons had reached manhood. Resolving to find their natural mother, whoever she might be, they set off, driving a donkey before them. On arriving at Tamarmara, in the kingdom of Kanesh, they asked the citizens to build up a fire for them in an upstairs room, making it warm for themselves and their donkey. "Since when," asked the Tamarmarans in wonder, "can a donkey climb a staircase?" The boys retorted scornfully, "Since when could a woman give birth to thirty children at a time? And yet our mother bore us all together after a single pregnancy!"

Their hosts were immediately seized by the spirit of competition: "Our Queen in Kanesh has borne thirty daughters at once," they replied indignantly. "She gave birth to thirty sons too, some time ago, but they disappeared." Immediately, the boys realized that they had found their mother. They went straight to Kanesh to see her, but the gods had changed their appearance so their mother failed to recognize them. It occurred to her that these thirty young strangers would make husbands for her thirty daughters, so she urged them to marry. But the thirtieth son said: "Should we really be taking our own sisters in marriage? It cannot be right for us to couple with them." And here the fragment ends.

Wrong and Right

The story of Appu and his two sons has a straightforward moral, which is stated unequivocally at the outset: "The god always vindicates the just, but he cuts down the wicked like trees, smashing the skulls of those who do wrong." A very wealthy man, Appu had everything he could have ever desired – all except a son or daughter to share his good fortune. One day, in despair, he went to see the Sun God to ask for his assistance. The Sun God asked Appu about his problem. "The gods have given me riches," he replied, "but I lack one thing: a son or a daughter." The Sun God looked on him kindly. "Go home and get drunk," he told Appu. "Go to bed with your wife and make love with her. The gods will give you a son."

Appu made his way home rejoicing, and everything happened just as the Sun God had predicted. His wife became pregnant, the months passed, and finally Appu had his longed-for son whom he decided to call Wrong. Not long afterward, Appu's wife became pregnant again. A second son was born, and Appu called him Right. The two boys grew up side by side, but when they reached manhood Wrong declared that he wanted to be independent. "Since the mountains dwell separately; since the rivers flow in separate courses … since the gods themselves live separately, we too should settle in different places," he said. The brothers began to divide up their father's estate. Wrong took one half, and gave the other half to Right. Wrong also made absolutely certain that he took the best ploughing ox for himself, giving the inferior cow to his guileless brother.

The Sun God, watching from his place in the heavens, saw what Wrong was doing. "Let Right's inferior cow become the best," he commanded. Then he ordered the brothers to be brought before him. He ensured that Right was fully compensated, and then condemned Wrong to be punished for his deed.

Kessi and his Beautiful Wife

As the gods ensured that justice was done between men, they were entitled to respect and fair treatment. Despite being incomplete, the story of the hunter Kessi and his beautiful wife contains a warning for anyone who might have been tempted to forget piety and neglect his duties towards the gods. Quite simply, the myth tells of how Kessi's infatuation with his wife Sintalimeni blinded him to all his other obligations. Instead of

To the Hittites cattle were vitally important, so Wrong's appropriation of his father's prize ox would have been considered highly significant. This gold cow was made c.1400–1200BC.

Hunting was a favourite pastime among kings, emphasizing their power and authority. Scenes such as the one depicted in this 11th-century Hittite relief show the hunt in full cry.

The Sun God and the Fisherman

One of the Hittites' most striking stories is the curious tale of the sun god, Simige and the fisherman. Only a small part of the original clay tablet has survived, and this is illegible in places. What remains, however, provides a revealing portrait of relations among the gods, animals and man – and affords an intriguing glimpse of the Hittites' wry humour as well as customs surrounding the arrival of new members of the family.

The Sun God looked down from the sky to see a cow grazing and was filled with desire. Descending to the Earth in the form of a young man, he accosted the cow and demanded to know by what right it grazed in his meadow. He then caught the cow and coupled with it, and nine months later the cow gave birth.

Shocked to discover that her calf had only two legs, the cow tried to kill and eat it, but the Sun God, watching from above, intervened. He seized his son, removed him to safety, stroked him tenderly and then left him on a grassy mound, surrounded by poisonous snakes as guards.

A childless fisherman happened to pass by. He rejoiced to find the baby he had so much longed for, and gave thanks to Simige for his good fortune. He took the child home, where his wife was equally delighted. Even in this moment of joy, however, they saw an opportunity to make profit: "Take this child into the bedroom, lie down on the bed and wail," said the fisherman to his wife. "The whole city will hear you and assume that you've given going off into the mountains to hunt, he lingered at home indulging in the pleasure of her company. Rather than providing for his mother's needs, he tended to Sintalimeni's every whim. Once he had worshipped the gods with dedication, making offerings and libations in their honour, but now his adoration was reserved for his wife alone.

His mother remonstrated with Kessi over his neglect of his duties until, finally, he acknowledged that it was time to go hunting again. Whistling for his dogs and taking up his spear, he ascended Mount Natara to see what he could find. To his surprise the woods were deserted; not an animal was in sight. Angered at the way Kessi had neglected their altars, the gods had hidden away all the game. For three months Kessi roamed the mountains, hunting ever more fruitlessly but reluctant to return home without anything to show for his expedition. He became increasingly weary, hungry and thirsty, and eventually fell seriously ill. Kessi lay down to rest beneath a tree, where, in his delirium, he had a series of seven unusual dreams. In one, he went out to hunt lions but instead found only serpents and sphinxes. Perplexed, he went to ask his mother the significance of these dreams. The inscription breaks off at this point, leaving the final outcome unclear. But the moral of the story could hardly be more apparent: no earthly attachment should be allowed to interfere with an individual's duty to the gods.

birth. Then one person will bring us bread, another will bring beer, and someone else will bring us fat."

Sure enough the community responded: "The fisherman's wife has had a baby!" the cry went up. The town flocked to the fisherman's house, and overwhelmed the couple with gifts.

The Sun God coupled with a cow and nine months later had to stop her from killing their newborn child.

HATTUSAS, CENTRE OF POWER

In *c.*1650BC Hattusilis I, the father of the Hittite Empire, chose the city of Hattusas as his capital. On a rise between two streams, the site was a natural stronghold, strategically placed near the junction of two major trade routes. A large double wall was constructed by the Hittites to complete its fortification. The city was a religious as a well as an administrative centre: there were some thirty temples within its boundaries and close by.

Left: Entry to Hattusas was by one of several gates, each of which was protected by fortifications to keep away human invaders and by carved figures to keep away supernatural ones. These two stone lions stand guard on the southwest of the city.

Below: Behind the remains of an ancient storehouse lie the ruins of the Great Temple, a huge square construction with sides 275m long. The king performed many of the most important public rituals here. The temple contained several rooms grouped around a courtyard. In the holiest of these were statues of two deities, probably Teshub and the Sun Goddess of Arinna, hidden from the view of ordinary worshippers.

Left: **This magnificent 2m high figure has lent his supposed identity to the so-called "King's Gate", although the carving probably represents a god.**

Below: **Several castles stand on high points of the city, like this one on a hill known as Yenicekale. They were erected as part of a defence system.**

Below and below left: **Just to the northeast of Hattusas are two natural chambers in an outcrop of rock that was probably a religious centre. The site, Yazilikaya, is remarkable for the depiction of the entire Hittite pantheon that lines the chamber walls.**

The Legacy of the Mesopotamians

The ancient civilizations of the Near East left behind them a dazzling inheritance, beginning with the construction of Sumer, some 5000 years ago in the valleys of what is now southern Iraq. They left to posterity an impressive string of achievements: the foundation of the first cities, the origins of writing and the first literary canon, the establishment of a code of law, and perhaps the first organized religion.

To the Christian West and its cultural descendants, the great legacy of the ancient Near East remained largely unappreciated until the nineteenth century. The foundations of once mighty cities had been hidden by shifting sands and the accomplishments of the vanished age were concealed by a great deal of negative publicity.

Almost everyone had heard of the Hanging Gardens of Babylon – although long vanished, they were, after all, one of the wonders of the ancient world – but Babylon, its predecessors and its contemporaries, were not generally considered in a favourable light by the outside world. Until the late nineteenth century, our only source of knowledge of the great civilizations in the Near East – with the exception of a few tantalizing Greek and Egyptian references – was the Old Testament. Of Sumer, the oldest culture of them all, there is virtually no mention in the Bible, although Abraham the Patriarch came from the Sumerian city of Ur, ancient even in his time.

The Hebrews did not admire their richer neighbours, the Sumerians, which may account for an absence of biblical references to them. The prophets found their polytheism deeply offensive; their relatively luxurious lifestyles were considered

According to the Book of Revelation the Whore of Babylon rode a scarlet beast with seven heads and ten horns. This 16th-century painting is by Lucas Cranach.

dangerously seductive and their military power was thought a serious threat. So with vituperative skill, they told the Hebrew story the way *they* saw it.

For instance, a great deal of space in the books of Judges and Kings, is devoted to the long struggle for ideological purity in opposition to the Canaanites who worshipped Baal. Apostasy is a recurring theme: "And they forsook the Lord, and served Baal and Ashtaroth." (Judges II, 13) The local gods, naturally enough, are uniformly presented as evil and oppressive; and Yahweh triumphs in the end. The intricacy of the old religion of Canaan was effectively obliterated by its Israelite successor until the excavation of Ugarit in the 1920s, and the deciphering of its ancient clay tablets over the following years.

This tower in Abu Dulaf near Samarra, Iraq, is influenced by ziggurat design which originated in ancient Sumer.

As for Babylon, the conquest of Jerusalem by its kings and the subsequent traumatic years of the Hebrew captivity within its walls influenced the prophets' writings. By the waters of Babylon, the Psalmist wept, "How shall we sing the Lord's song in a strange land?" Of the Old Testament's hundreds of references to the city, some are neutral but few are favourable and many are scathing. It is with a great deal of satisfaction that Isaiah writes, "Babylon is fallen, is fallen; and all the graven images of her gods he hath broken into the ground." (Isaiah XXI, 9)

The Book of Revelation in the New Testament upholds Babylon as the ultimate example of the wicked city: "Babylon the great, the mother of harlots and abominations of the Earth." (Revelation XVII, 5) The author, Saint John the Divine, was actually referring to Rome, considered a den of iniquity in the eyes of the early Christians. In any case the apocalyptic text of the Book of Revelation has long defied unambiguous interpretation. Nonetheless, Babylon's bad reputation was sealed.

In Christian Europe, until modern times, Babylon has therefore symbolized corruption and irreligion. Isaiah's words, "Babylon is fallen", served as a slogan for the Parliamentary soldiers of the English Civil War, a battle-chant that pre cipitated revolutionary change. To this day, extreme Protestant groups loudly denounce the Catholic Church with references to "the Whore of Babylon".

Although this perception of Babylon is far removed from the reality of Near Eastern civilization, it is so entrenched that even the beginnings of serious archaeology in the region, toward the end of the nineteenth century, seemed unable to counteract more than two thousand years of calumny. When film director D. W. Griffiths made his colossal epic *Intolerance* in 1916, his Babylonian sets were rich with architectural detail taken meticulously from recent excavations; but the depraved decadence of his story was straight from the Revelation of Saint John.

The discoveries made by archaeologists, however, provided an enormously exciting story in their own right. Until the 1880s, excavators in Mesopotamia had been more intent on pillaging ruins for trophies or inscriptions than on preserving or even understanding the monuments they came from. Things changed for the better in 1886, when a German team led by Robert Koldewey applied a new, scientific method called stratigraphy to their digs. By cutting deep into the ground and uncovering successive layers, a team could gradually uncover a site's history and ascertain the antiquity of their finds.

The dig undertaken by Americans at Nippur began in 1889 and took twelve years despite appalling living conditions and occasional attacks from local bandits. It was less precise than the German excavations but was still enormously productive: no less than 30,000 tablets containing everything from literature to the equivalent of domestic lists were made available to scholars struggling to master the intricacies of a long-dead language written in a forgotten script.

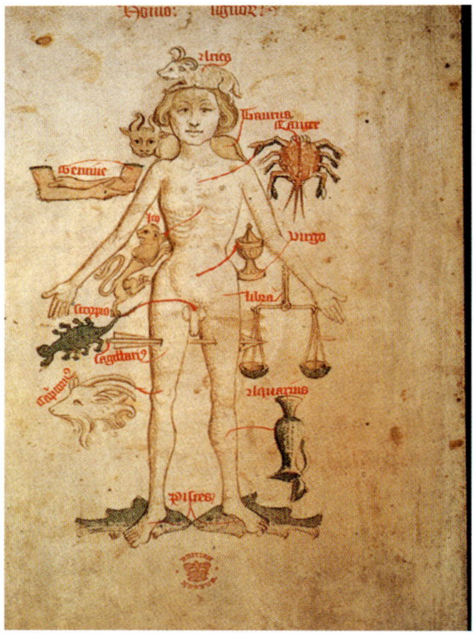

The twelve Mesopotamian signs of the Zodiac were appropriated by the West. This 15th-century figure shows the signs' associations with parts of the body.

At Ur, in the 1920s and 30s, the British archaeologist Leonard Woolley showed just what could be achieved. Eventually, he reconstructed a history of the city that went back to its days as an agricultural settlement in around 5500BC. Most spectacularly, he was able to reveal to an increasingly astonished public the royal tombs of Ur, where there is evidence to suggest that ancient kings might have been buried with a retinue of sacrificed servants to accompany them into the next world.

The secret of Woolley's method was patience. Where previous excavators had often succeeded only in exposing ancient structures both to the weather and the depredations of local builders intent on recycling 4000-year-old bricks, he spent years training himself and his labour force before opening sites. The rewards were great, not least in popular understanding: it was not long after Woolley's first reconstruction of the ziggurat of Ur, for example, that the ziggurat design began to make its appearance as an art deco motif. Woolley's excavations (among the digs of others) did a great deal topopularize archaeologists, giving them the image of an heroic exponent of the rich but long-forgotten past.

Yet, even before scholars came to translate cuneiform texts, some of the "Babylonian" legacy had been appropriated. The technologies developed in Mesopotamia for irrigation and flood control had been in widespread use for thousands of years. The 360-degree circle and the sexagesimal measurement first developed by the Sumerians, is still used to denote units of time today. This system of measurement also divided the heavens into the twelve zodiacal signs – the basis for the practice of astrology.

But it was the writings that made clear the stupendous extent of the Mesopotamian inheritance. It is scarcely an exaggeration to claim that almost every myth and legend found around the Mediterranean world has some kind of Akkadian or Sumerian parallel. The Epic of Gilgamesh and its associated poems (see pages 74–93) include episodes and subplots found in much subsequent Greek mythology, from the descent of Orpheus into the Underworld to the wanderings of Odysseus. The Anzu bird befriended by Lugalbanda (pages 72–73) has much in common with the roc of the *Arabian Nights*. Even the bull-cult of Minoan Crete may have been linked to the sacred bulls of Mesopotamia.

Like the legends – most of which in any case had pointed morals – religious ideas also diffused across the area from the original Sumerian source. Individual gods and goddesses appear to undergo a gentle transformation as they move across from one culture to the next. Thus Inana, goddess of Uruk, clearly shares similar characteristics with Ashtart and Anat, who in turn are associated with the Greek Pallas Athene or perhaps even to the great Diana of the Ephesians, the many-breasted goddess whose adulators aroused the venom of Saint Paul in the Acts of the Apostles.

Indeed, the Hebrew Bible itself, the great excoriator of the idolators, owes something to the Mesopotamian world. Knowledge gleaned from Ugaritic texts has cast much light on early Hebrew.

The two languages are not so very different, but the most startling discoveries relate to the development of what was to become a distinctly Jewish monotheism. Although the idea would certainly have appalled the prophets of Israel, it seems clear that El, the Ugaritic and Canaanite father-god, displays a number of characteristics typical of Yahweh, and can even be seen as an evolutionary precursor of Israel's Jehovah.

El also has much in common with Enlil, Sumer's "king of Heaven and Earth". Many other Sumerian and Akkadian themes are present throughout the Old Testament: the most obvious example being the tales of the flood (see pages 86–88) which find their way into Genesis.

Possibly the most striking similarity between Mesopotamian religion and the Old Testament is in the concept of a God or the gods choosing to punish impiety with catastrophe. Yahweh repeatedly scourges the Israelites with invasion and slaughter at the hands of the Philistines or indeed the Babylonians, depending on who is available and the extent of the people's crimes. In just the same way, Enlil chastises the great city of Agade by conjuring up an invading horde of murderous nomads, who duly raze it to the ground.

It may be that tales are always recycled and passed on from one civilization to the next. The Mesopotamians and their neighbours recorded them first, just as they created most of the necessities of civilization, from agricultural surplus to law, from kingship and administrative bureaucracy to a comfortable urban architecture. Their ultimate legacy may well have been civilized life itself.

When D. W. Griffiths created the scenery for his Babylonian epic *Intolerance* in 1916, he made certain that the sets reproduced the ancient architecture down to the smallest detail. This particular still shows a crowd among the colossal columns of the city's great banqueting hall.

Glossary of Key Terms and Deities

Mesopotamian deities often have several names according to geography or historical developments. Unless otherwise indicated the names below are those most commonly used.

Adad the god of rain who was instructed by **Enlil** to cause a drought and exterminate the whole of humankind

Akkadian ancient language of Babylon

An (Anu) literally "sky" or "heavens", a remote deity who controlled kingship and cosmic laws

Anat the Ugaritic goddess of sexual love and fertility

Anzu bird the terrifying lion-headed bird that was persuaded by **Lugalbanda** to grant him a wish

Apsu the god who personified the primordial fresh waters and gave them their name

Assyrians northern Mesopotamian people who dominated the region from 883–612BC

Azag a mighty monster which was a kind of stone. It caused landslides and had to be conquered by **Ninurta**

Baal (Hadad) "lord", a title used in different Canaanite cities to refer to their own, particular tutelary deity

Bull of Heaven a mythical beast commanded by **Inana** to destroy Uruk because **Gilgamesh** had refused her advances

cuneiform the earliest form of writing created by pressing wedge-shaped reeds into wet clay

Dumuzi the shepherd god who was the lover of **Inana**

El Ugaritic father of the gods, he was remote and authoritarian, similar to **Anu**

Enki (Ea) the cunning craftsman of the gods associated with water, irrigation canals and fertility

Enkidu the wild man created to oppose **Gilgamesh**. The two foes eventually became great companions

Enlil (Ellil) a powerful and aggressive warrior deity who manifested in violent storms and fostered the growth of crops

Enmerkar a king who features in the **Gilgamesh** cycle. He was said to have built the first walls of Uruk

Enuma elish the best-known version of Mesopotamian creation myths which dates from as early as 1900–1200BC

Ereshkigal the goddess of the Underworld, sister to **Inana**

***galla* demons** spirits created by the gods as weapons of war

Geshtin-ana (Bellili) the sister of the shepherd **Dumuzi**. She interpreted her brother's dream, prophesying his death

Gilgamesh a great warrior, ruler, lover and demi-god who features in a cycle of myths about the unsuccessful quest for immortality

Hittites the people of ancient Anatolia

Huwawa the forest monster hunted down by **Gilgamesh** and **Enkidu**

Igigi gods the Sumerian sky gods who helped to create irrigation canals

Illuyanka the Earth serpent that features in Hittite myths

Inana (Ashtart, Astarte, Ishtar) goddess of sexual love associated with the city of Uruk

Kumarbi the Hittite father of the gods

Lugalbanda a king of Uruk who was divinely favoured and thought to be the father of **Gilgamesh**

Lugale a poem that narrates the battle between **Ninurta**, god of the thunderstorm, and the **Azag** monster

Marduk the great god of Babylon who was superlative in every way

me cosmic powers or properties of the gods that enabled civilized existence

Mot the Ugaritic god of death

Nanna (Suen, Sin) the moon god, son of **Enlil** and **Ninlil**

Nergal the lover of **Ereshkigal** who came to rule with her in the Underworld

Ninhursaga (Ninmah, Mami) the goddess who represented motherhood

Ninlil the goddess of young corn who gave birth to the moon

Ninurta a warrior god who controlled the thunderstorm, the flood and the plough. He was the son of **Enlil**

Pazuzu an Underworld demon often depicted with a canine face and scaly body

Pukku-mekku a game played at weddings that involved a puck and a stick. When **Gilgamesh** was searching for his lost puck he discovered the Underworld

Qingu a warrior god given the **Tablet of Destinies** by **Tiamat** on whose behalf he fought. Later the gods captured him and used his blood to create humankind

Simige the Hittite sun god

Sin-lege-unninni the scribe and scholar said to have recorded the version of the **Gilgamesh** epic (*c.*1100BC) which has survived until today

Sumerians the ancient people of southern Mesopotamia who invented writing and created the earliest-known civilization on Earth (*c.*3500BC)

Tablet of Destinies a **cuneiform** tablet belonging to **Enlil** which guaranteed his position as ruler of the universe and was said to confer the power to determine the destinies of the world

Teshub the all-conquering Hittite storm god

Tiamat the goddess who personified the primordial salt waters

Ubelluri the Hittite god who bore the whole Earth on his shoulders

Ugarit a city on the Mediterranean coast that is of great archaeological significance

Ut-napishti (Atra-hasis, Adapa) "He who found life", the only human being to find immortal life after a great flood. (He may have been the origin of the biblical Noah.)

Utu (Shamash) the sun god who made footprints on the ground that **Enki** filled with fresh water

Yamm the Ugaritic sea god, son of the god **El** and brother of **Baal**

Ziggurat a rectangular tower surmounted by a temple

For More Information

Department of Near Eastern Studies
Cornell University
409 White Hall
Ithaca, NY 14853
(607)-255-6275
Website: neareasternstudies.cornell.edu
The Department of Near Eastern Studies at Cornell University offers courses on a wide array of subjects important for understanding the full sweep of Near Eastern civilizations.

Department of Near Eastern Studies
Princeton University
Princeton, NJ 08544
(609) 258-4280
Website: www.princeton.edu/nes
Founded as the Department of Oriental Languages and Literatures, the Department of Near Eastern Studies focuses on medieval and pre-modern studies of the geographical area that includes the Arab lands, Iran, Israel, and Turkey, as well as the modern Muslim world in its entirety, including the Caucasus, Central Asia, South Asia, and Southeast Asia.

Department of Near Eastern Studies
University of California, Berkeley
250 Barrows Hall
Berkeley, CA 94720-1940
(510) 642-3757
Website: nes.berkeley.edu
Founded in 1894, Berkeley's Near Eastern Studies Department, is one of the oldest and most distinguished such departments in the country.

Department of Middle Eastern and Islamic Studies
New York University
50 Washington Square South
New York, NY 10012
(212) 998-8880
Website: meis.as.nyu.edu
The Department of Middle Eastern and Islamic Studies at New York University offers an undergraduate major (and minor) as well as a graduate program leading to the Ph.D.

Websites

Because of the changing nature of Internet links, Rosen Publishing has developed an online list of websites related to the subject of this book. This site is updated regularly. Please use this link to access the list:

http://www.rosenlinks.com/COW/neast

For Further Reading

Dalley, Stephanie. *Myths from Mesopotamia: Creation, the Flood, Gilgamesh, and Others*. Oxford, England: Oxford University Press, 2000.

Firdawsi, Dick Davis, and Azar Nafisi. *Shahnameh: The Persian Book of Kings*. New York, NY: Penguin, 2016.

Fullman. *Ancient Civilizations*. London, England: DK, 2013.

Herodotus, Tom Holland, and Paul Cartledge. *The Histories*. New York, NY: Penguin, 2015.

Kriwaczek, Paul. *Babylon: Mesopotamia and the Birth of Civilization*. New York, NY: Thomas Dunne /St. Martin's, 2012.

Lassieur, Allison. *Ancient Mesopotamia*. New York, NY: Children's Press, 2012.

McLaughlin, John L. *The Ancient Near East: An Essential Guide*. Nashville, TN: Abingdon, 2012.

Mehta-Jones, Shilpa. *Life in Ancient Mesopotamia*. New York, NY: Crabtree, 2005.

Mitchell, Stephen. *Gilgamesh: A New English Version*. New York, NY: Free Press, 2004.

Oakes, Lorna. *Mesopotamia: All about Ancient Assyria and Babylonia, with 15 Step-by-step Projects and More than 300 Exciting Pictures*. London, England: Armadillo, 2012.

Steele, Philip. *Eyewitness Mesopotamia*. London, England: DK, 2007.

Index

Page numbers in italic denote captions. Where there is a textual reference to the topic on the same page as a caption, italics have not been used.

Picture Credits

Key: a above; **b** below; **c** centre; **l** left; **r** right

Abbreviations:

AAA	Ancient Art and Architecture Collection
AKG	AKG, London
AKG/EL	Erich Lessing, AKG
BAL	Bridgeman Art Library
CMD	Mike Dixon
ETA	e.t. archive
MH	Michael Holford
GDO	Giovanni dagli Orti, France

Title page ETA; **Contents page** GDO; **6** George Gerster/Comstock; **7** GDO; **8l** Robert Harding Picture Library; **8** George Gerster/Comstock; **9** MH; **10** GDO; **12l** AKG; **12b** British Museum; **13ar** ETA; **13bl** ETA; **13bc** ETA; **13br** MH; **14** GDO; **15** GDO; **16** GDO; **17** GDO; **18al** MH; **18bl** AKG/EL; **18r** MH; **19l** GDO; **19r** ETA; **20** ETA; **21** CMD; **22** AAA; **23** MH; **24** CMD; **26** Dieter Hoppe/AKG; **28** CMD; **29** Hutchison Library; **30** GDO; **31** MH; **32** George Gerster/Comstock; **36** MH; **37** ETA; **39** ETA; **40** AKG/EL; **41** AAA; **42** ETA; **43** AAA; **44** Comstock; **45** AKG/EL; **46** ETA; **47** ETA; **48** ETA; **50** ETA; **51** Hutchison Library; **52** GDO; **53** AKG/EL; **54** MH; **56** MH; **57** AKG/EL; **58** AKG/EL; **59al** CMD; **59ar** MH; **59b** ETA; **60** ETA; **61al** BAL; **65ar** AKG/EL; **61b** ETA; **62** ETA; **63** AAA; **64** Hutchison Library; **65** AKG/EL; **66** George Gerster/Comstock; **67** British Museum; **68** MH; **69** ETA; **70** AKG/EL; **71** ETA; **74** BAL; **75** MH; **76** AKG/EL; **77** British Museum; **78** MH; **79** MH; **80** AKG/EL; **82** MH; **84** MH; **85** AKG/EL; **86** CMD; **87** MH; **89** ETA; **90–91b** George Gerster/Comstock; **91a** GDO; **93** BAL; **94l** ETA; **94r** CMD; **94b** ETA; **95l** British Museum; **95r** AKG/EL; **95b** ETA; **96** ETA; **97** GDO; **98** GDO; **99** MH; **100** CMD; **102** ETA; **104** GDO; **105** GDO; **107** Panos Pictures; **108** MH; **110** British Museum; **111** GDO; **114** AKG/EL; **115** GDO; **116–117** Sonia Halliday Photographs; **118** AKG/EL; **119** CMD; **120** ETA; **122** F. H. C. Birch/Sonia Halliday Photographs; **123** Werner Forman Archive,; **124** Hutchison Library; **126** GDO; **127** GDO; **128–129a** ETA; **128b** GDO; **129b** ETA; **132** ETA; **134** AKG/EL; **135** Hutchison Library; **136** ETA; **137** The Kobal Collection.